GW01252163

THE PLANTARY COOKBOOK

THE PLANTARY COOKBOOK

Modular, vegan meals
that taste great

Ellen Barrett

Copyright © 2023 by Ellen Barrett

All rights reserved.

*This hardback edition first
published in November 2023*

*All Images Copyright, Ellen Barrett,
except cover photo by Chris Barrett
and images by Pixabay users
5526837 (pg 12) and 12138562
(pg 47), and Unsplash user
@elloproducts (pg 18)*

*ISBN: 978-1-916972-00-1 (Hardback)
ISBN: 978-1-916972-01-8 (Paperback)
ISBN: 978-1-916972-02-5 (e-book)*

*Published by Quirky Ink
QuirkyInk.co.uk*

To my younger self, who
I aim to make proud,
and to my family who
continues to support my
curiosity, interests and
love for food

TABLE OF CONTENTS

INTRODUCTION

HOW IT ALL STARTED

LET ME INTRODUCE YOU TO THE PART OF ME THAT HASN'T CHANGED

BEING VEGAN

Growing up, I was inspired by close friends that were vegetarian or vegan and I learnt a lot about what they care about, be it the environment, animals, and ultimately humans. In lockdown, I took time (with plenty of it) to experiment with vegan cooking, starting with banana bread of course. I had a lot of fun with it and felt comfortable enough to became vegan.

My first university year was mainly in lockdown so I'd be lying if I said I felt up to making delicious, nutritious meals 3 times a day. In reality, I had many a depressing bowl of pesto pasta - (unlike my new and improved recipe - Punchy Pesto and Green Bean Pasta on page 78) and often had breakfast at 3pm.

The following year, I launched my Instagram account, @the.plantary_, with the goal of sharing easy and delicious vegan recipes for students. As I create this cookbook, I'm reminded of why I'm on this journey. Veganism is the 'single biggest way' to reduce our environmental impact[1]. I'm vegan because I believe in walking the talk. For the last 3 years, I've studied Psychology and Sustainability. I've come to understand the profound consequences of our actions on the planet, alongside the nuanced challenges associated with driving behavioural change.

1   *Independent 24 September 2020*

But with
community
and connection,
all the more is
possible.

This cookbook aims to make
vegan cooking accessible
with every recipe, making
it easy for everyone to
'plant' their forks into something
scrumptious. I hope to make people
feel welcome to vegan cooking
and to foster a community
where the joy of creating and
savouring delicious food is
shared.

A MODULAR APPROACH

In the film Ratatouille, Auguste Gusteau says, "Anyone can cook." While I agree with this sentiment, cooking can sometimes feel overwhelming and time-consuming. Hence, I wanted my cookbook to be 'modular'.

Mix, match, master: this book is your

substitute and repurp

Substitute ingredients to match your budget and tastes

The book is made for modularity. Each recipe features a 'Finer Detail' section that suggests component swaps. A component is an element of the dish like the carbohydrate base or the protein source that can be substituted based on what you already have, and in alignment with your own goals: to meet nutritional targets, to avoid allergens, to budget, or to save time on cooking.

Repurpose recipe components to minimise food waste

Ingredients that you won't use up in one recipe can be repurposed and used in others. For example, after making a curry or a dip that uses chickpeas, you can then save the aquafaba (the liquid from a tin of chickpeas) and use it as an egg replacement in my Chocolate Chunk Cookie recipe (page 152).

Batch make components, and use them with versatility

Some components have their own separate recipes so you might make them in batches and use them for different meals throughout the week. For example, my punchy pesto recipe uses up leftover spinach and can be used in a classic pesto pasta, on top of soups and salads or as a sandwich spread.

INGREDIENTS AND SUBSTITUTIONS

TOFU

Tofu is highly adaptable. Silken tofu is my favourite way to blend in protein and a creamy texture to sauces. Firm tofu can be crumbled to make a scramble or marinated to soak up flavours. You can even freeze tofu and thaw it for a chewy texture that I enjoy in sandwiches.

See: maple french toast, smashed avocados and scramble bagels, eggless mayo baguettes, the Flatwich, spaghetti carbonara, crispy tofu ramen, and Vietnamese noodle bowl.

NUTRITIONAL YEAST

The bearer of vitamin B12 and a cheesy, umami flavour. Perfect for cheesy sauces or sprinkled over pasta and salads.

See: eggless mayo baguettes, smashed avocados and scramble bagels, caesar salad and almost every pasta dish.

AQUAFABA

Aquafaba is the liquid from tinned chickpeas and a surprisingly effective egg substitute in baking.

See: Anum's chocolate chunk cookies and classic banana bread.

BANANA BLOSSOM

Banana blossom mimics the texture of seafood and, when coated with batter, makes a mean component of 'fish and chips'.

See: 'Fish n' chips'.

GARLIC SALT

This is a personal favourite seasoning of mine. My friends buy it for me in bulk and my mother hides it from me. You are welcome to choose your side freely, but know its power. When paired with nutritional yeast in a pasta dish, the result is cheesy, salty, garlic goodness.

See: almost every savoury recipe.

GARNISHES

· Grated vegan cheese
· Spring onions
· Dry roasted peanuts
· Sesame seeds
· Coriander
· Parsley

VEGAN MEAT

Vegan substitutes for meat and dairy products have become much more popular in supermarkets in the last few years. Though I still love to experiment with tofu, tempeh, banana blossom, jackfruit, beans and mushrooms, I do have a few trusted brands of plant-based meats. However, they are not always the most affordable option and veganism should be accessible to all. So, below I have included some examples of good substitutes I favour.

Vegan chicken - Oyster mushrooms have a meaty texture and can be used for vegan "fried chicken", otherwise tofu torn into pieces or cut into fillets work well with cornflour as a chicken substitute

Vegan sausages - when combined with oats and spices, cooked lentils can be shaped into sausages to cook from scratch.

Vegan bacon - aubergine, sliced thinly and seasoned with smoky flavourings like liquid smoke, BBQ sauce and paprika can be baked or fried until crispy.

Tofu - to avoid soy or for a cheaper option, butter beans or chickpeas can be mashed up or used whole for texture.

MINIMISING FOOD WASTE

60% of UK food waste comes from the home†

General rules to follow

Use what you already have

Select meals based on what needs to be used up. Substitute ingredients rather than buying more, plan ahead and only buy what you need.

Prime yourself to eat in the right order

Check "use by" dates and put older items at the front of your fridge (similar to in supermarkets), so you're more likely to use them sooner. Recipe plan to have the meals with more perishable items to be used first.

Freeze what you won't get through before its use by

A common example is bread that you can then just defrost in the toaster. Often meals can be frozen and saved for later too! When defrosted, it's best to only reheat the food once, so divide your leftovers into portions before freezing.

Share items with friends or flatmates

It might be that you already share your supermarket delivery with your flatmates, but have you considered splitting a loaf, a block of tofu, or even a head of broccoli? Not only are you more likely to reduce food waste but you'll also save money.

Compost what you can

Food practices need to be circular, and regenerative, not just sustainable, and composting is a great working example of this. Consider starting a compost heap at home, and add to it each time you cook, to dispose of food scraps and enrich your garden soil.

Other ideas

Spinach can be wilted in a pan towards the end of cooking or added to smoothies and sauces.

Leftover burger buns can be blended into breadcrumbs to go on top of any pasta dish (particularly Aglio e Olio on page 84).

Eat peels and skins - from carrots to kiwis and even bananas, these can all be eaten if prepared properly (be mindful, as for instance green potato skin can be poisonous). Cut or peel the stem of the broccoli and cook as normal.

Know the difference between "best before" and "use by". There is no need to throw out food that is past its "best before" date; before "use by" is safe to eat.

† source: Hall, M. (2022). Food waste 2023 The facts. [online] Business Waste

HOW TO READ THE RECIPES

Recipes are sized to feed two hungry eaters

A brief **description** of the dish, sometimes featuring a dedication

Sub-headings within the ingredients list to show the different components of the dish

Tips on **substitutions** for budgeting and flavour preferences

Points on how to alter the taste and texture of the dish

Personal product **recommendations**

BLACK FOREST SMOOTHIE BOWL

A thick cherry and chocolate smoothie you can scoop into a bowl with toppings galore

INGREDIENTS

FOR THE SMOOTHIE
250g frozen **cherries**
1 frozen **banana**
1 scoop (30g) chocolate flavoured **protein powder**
120ml **plant milk**

FOR THE TOPPINGS
1 **banana**
30g **walnuts**
20g homemade **granola**†

FINER DETAIL

Using frozen fruit and toppings like sliced banana and batch-baked granola helps keep this dish more affordable. Fresh cherries and cacao nibs would be a delicious but more expensive alternative.

If you only have plain or vanilla flavoured protein powder, add the same quantity but with an additional tsp of cocoa powder.

This smoothie is designed to be thick, to be eaten with a spoon. If you prefer it thinner, you can use fresh banana/add more plant milk.

I've found sweetened vegan oat milk works best with this recipe, but experiment to your heart's content.

44

† recipe on page 54

METHOD

1. To a blender, add the **smoothie ingredients** and blend until well combined. A strong blender should be able to do this in one go but, if weaker, pour the milk in slowly and add a little more than the recipe calls for if needed.

2. Pour the mixture into a bowl

3. Slice the **banana** into thin coins and roughly chop the **walnuts**

4. Gently place the banana slices on top of the smoothie, then sprinkle on the walnuts and **granola** ready to serve!

Reference to other recipes that complement the dish as an added **component**

A **numbered method** section with detailed but comprehensive steps.

Ingredients used are in bold to help you identify what to use when

Calorie and **protein** measurements, per serving - unless otherwise stated, are included to inform personal nutrition goals

Prep time. Some recipes also detail the additional time needed for baking, oven cooking, refrigeration, proofing etc.

Serving size information specifying the number of servings or pieces it yields

Every single recipe includes a **large, clear photo** of the dish. I argue this is a non-negotiable feature for any cookbook, but if you're new to vegan cooking seeing the final result is particularly important

Protein (g) 12.7
Calories (kcal) 306

15 mins

Serves 2

45

THE PLANTARY CHEAT SHEET

In many of the recipes, the method asks to "cook to packet instructions". Depending on what pasta, noodle or rice type etc. you have chosen, they are likely to call for different cooking times. However, below I provide a general guide to cooking times, along with definitions to key phrases I adopt or indeed invent.

COOK TO PACKET INSTRUCTIONS

Rice: 1 part rice to 1 part water. Wash and drain the rice to clean it and remove the surface starch to separate the grains and make it fluffier. Bring to the boil, then cook on low heat for 20 minutes with a tea towel under the lid (to absorb any condensation from the boiling). This will work for sushi rice too.

Quinoa: 1 part quinoa to 2 parts vegetable broth. Rinse the quinoa to remove the saponin (its bitter coating). Bring the quinoa and stock to a boil, then reduce to a simmer and cook for 15 minutes until the liquid has been absorbed. Fluff with a fork and serve.

Noodles: 1 part noodles to 4 parts water. If the recipe calls for the noodles to be cooked separately, bring the water to a boil and cook for 3-6 minutes (ramen usually take 3-4 and rice noodles 5-6). Drain, rinse with cold water and set aside while you cook the other components.

Pasta: 1 part pasta to 2 parts water. Bring the water to the boil with a little salt to enhance the flavour. Add the pasta. Stir immediately and drizzle in a little oil to prevent sticking. Most pastas take between 8-10 minutes to cook.

Frying tofu: 2 tbsp of cornflour for 200g of tofu. Press the tofu to remove excess moisture by placing it between paper towels or clean kitchen towels and squeezing hard. You can even place something heavy on top of it and leave it for half an hour. Next, tear the tofu into small bite-sized pieces and coat with cornflour by rolling them on a shallow plate, or shaking both together in a tupperware. Lastly, fry the tofu pieces in a pan with enough oil to cover the bottom of the pan until golden brown - this typically takes 5-7 minutes.

Melting chocolate: To microwave: 4 parts chocolate to 1 part coconut oil. Chop the chocolate into small, evenly sized pieces, then microwave on low heat in short 15-30 second intervals, stirring at each break.
To double boil: Add the chocolate in a heatproof bowl. Bring a saucepan with a couple of inches of water to a simmer. Place the bowl on top of the saucepan, and allow the steam to melt the chocolate, stirring constantly.

Add a drizzle of oil: In some recipes I mention a drizzle of oil in the method section that is not included in the ingredients list. This is because the amount is fairly arbitrary and I assume most kitchens have cooking oil, so add the quantity that works best for your tastes and the pan you use (e.g. non-stick vs stainless steel.)

COMMUNITY

I've always loved my food. My dad taught me to cook when I struggled to hold a wooden spoon. I'm a firm believer that "no person is an island." So, I'd like to give credit to all the friends and family who have shared and supported my passion for food.

Community is a beautiful thing. I think of: cooking with my family; sharing ingredients with neighbours; the online social media community; discovering meals from my friends' families of different cultures; and hysterical late night baking sessions with flatmates.

To my community, whose different paths of life have happily crossed with mine, thank you. I have chosen to show my thanks by naming several of my recipes after those who have inspired them. You know who you are :))

And to you, reader, I encourage you to invest in your community. Reciprocity is basically innate and, arguably, the reason humankind have made it this far - though we still have a long way to go. Buying food is one way, having a cooking rota with flatmates is another, and of course following my Instagram @the. plantary_ is yet another ;))

But that's enough chit chat, lets get to the fooooood.

OATS

CHOCOLATE AND COCONUT OVERNIGHT OATS

INGREDIENTS

FOR THE OATS

2 cups **oats**

2½ cups **oat milk**

2 tbsp **desiccated coconut**

1 tbsp **coconut sugar** or **brown sugar**

FOR THE CHOCOLATE SHELL

120g **vegan chocolate** (chips or chopped)

FINER DETAIL

Using jars initially allows you to store portions until you need them.

Add 1-2 tbsp of chia seeds for added thickness and nutrition.

Sprinkle on some extra desiccated coconut in the morning, along with some agave syrup for extra sweetness.

METHOD

FOR THE OATS

1. For 2 jars, pour in each: 1 cup of **oats**, 1¼ cups of **oat milk**, 1 tbsp of **desiccated coconut**, and half a tbsp of **coconut sugar**

2. Screw on the lid and shake well

3. Leave in the fridge overnight to thicken

FOR THE CHOCOLATE SHELL

4. The next day, melt the **chocolate**

5. Pour the melted chocolate equally into the jars (or bowls) then add to the fridge or freezer for about 10 minutes before cracking into and enjoying

BANANA AND BISCOFF BAKED OATS

Baked oats went viral on Instagram for months for good reason! Made to make your winter mornings, creamy oatmeal cuddles a spoon of Biscoff spread baked to perfection then topped with banana slices.

INGREDIENTS

2 **bananas** (one for mashing, one for slicing)

½ cup **oats**

1 scoop (30g) **protein powder**

½ tsp **bicarbonate of soda**

½ cup **plant milk**

2 tsp **Biscoff spread**

FINER DETAIL

If you like this even sweeter, top with a little sugar or maple syrup.

For protein powder, Biscoff or 'Speculoos' flavour is best, but I've also found salted caramel or vanilla to work well too.

METHOD

1. Preheat the oven to 180°C

2. Mash one **banana** in a bowl, and stir in the **oats**, **protein power** (I used Protein Work's vegan salted caramel), and **bicarbonate of soda**

3. Once combined, pour in your **plant milk** of choice and stir

4. Pour half the mixture into an oven-safe dish for each person

5. Spoon your **Biscoff spread** into the middle, then pour in the rest of the mixture and bake in the oven for 10-15 minutes

6. Slice the second banana into coin slices, and add to the top

CARAMELISED APPLE OATS

INGREDIENTS

FOR THE CARAMELISED APPLE

1 medium **apple**

2 tbsp **vegan butter**

2 tbsp **brown sugar**

½ tsp **ground cinnamon**

A pinch of **salt**

FOR THE OATS

2 cups **plant milk**

1 cup **oats**

1 tbsp **maple syrup**

FINER DETAIL

Batch cook the oatmeal for breakfasts made ahead. Store the oats and caramelised apple separately and both should last 3-4 days

Add pecans or walnuts at the same time as the apples for extra indulgence

METHOD

FOR THE CARAMELISED APPLE

1. Dice the **apple**
2. Melt the **vegan butter** in a small frying pan on medium heat
3. Add the diced apple, **brown sugar**, **ground cinnamon**, and a pinch of **salt** to the pan
4. Cook the mixture, stirring to prevent burning, for about 5-7 minutes or until they soften and caramelise. Set aside while you make the oats

FOR THE OATS

5. In a saucepan, combine the **plant milk** of choice with the **oats** and bring to a simmer on a medium heat
6. Reduce the heat and cook for a further 5 minutes, stirring often to prevent sticking
7. Stir in the **maple syrup** to sweeten the oats

TO SERVE

8. Pour the oats into bowls to serve and spoon on the apple mixture

BERNIE'S CHOCCY OATS

Protein (g)	38	**10** mins
Calories (kcal)	380	

Serves 2

This recipe is dedicated to my niece. It was our breakfast every morning for a solid month in lockdown, and if choccy oats failed to brighten my day, she always did.

INGREDIENTS

2 cups **plant milk**

2 scoops (60g) chocolate **protein powder**

1 cup **oats**

50g **strawberries**

2 tbsp **chocolate sauce**, **spread** or **syrup**

FINER DETAIL

The protein powder I've found to taste the least like protein powder is from ProteinWorks (chocolate silk flavour for this recipe). Per scoop you get 25g of protein for 100 calories!

METHOD

1. Shake together the **plant milk** and **protein powder** in a jar, then heat in a saucepan until the mixture is gently simmering

2. Add the **oats** and stir to the desired thickness - roughly ten minutes

3. Spoon the oats into a bowl and top with **strawberries** and **chocolate sauce**, **spread** or **syrup**

BRUNCH

THE FLATWICH

INGREDIENTS

200g firm **tofu**

2 **tomatoes**

1 **avocado**

1 head **baby gem lettuce**

4 slices **bread**

vegan butter to spread

2 tbsp **vegan mayonnaise**

1 tbsp **sriracha**

FOR THE MARINADE

1 tbsp **soy sauce**

1 tbsp **maple syrup**

1 tsp **liquid smoke**

1 tsp **paprika**

½ tsp **garlic granules**

¼ tsp **black pepper**

FINER DETAIL

I like to have a side salad to use up any remaining salad veggies. Mix in the marinade bowl with a little extra soy sauce or balsamic vinegar.

METHOD

1. Preheat the oven to 180°C
2. Drain the **tofu** and cut into rasher-like slices, then place them on a lined baking tray
3. To make the marinade, simply mix all the **marinade ingredients** in a small bowl
4. Brush half the marinade onto the top faces of the tofu rashers and cook for 10 minutes
5. Meanwhile, cut the **tomato** and **avocado** into slices and roughly chop the **lettuce**
6. Toast the **bread**, and spread vegan **butter** if desired. Mix together the **mayo** and **sriracha** and spread onto the toasted bread
7. Remove the tray from the oven, flip over the tofu rashers, and brush on the final coating of the marinade
8. Bake for another 10 minutes until the tofu rashers are a maroon colour and crispy

TO SERVE

9. Lastly, layer the lettuce, tomato, tofu rashers and avocado onto the bread and close the sandwich. Cut the sandwiches in half and serve

MAPLE FRENCH TOAST

Protein (g)   8
Calories (kcal)   187

20 mins

Serves 2

Fuel your mornings with a unique twist: maple and banana are paired with the imposter ingredient of silken tofu for protein, potassium and pizzazz!

INGREDIENTS

¼ cup **plant milk**

150g **silken tofu**

1 tbsp **brown sugar**

1 tbsp **maple syrup**

1 tsp **cinnamon**

4 slices **bread**

a knob of **vegan butter**

FOR THE TOPPING

a knob of **vegan butter**

1 tbsp **icing sugar**

1 **banana,** sliced

1 tbsp **maple syrup**

FINER DETAIL

The tofu replaces egg (don't worry it's tasteless) and adds protein to your brunch!

The wet mixture lasts for a few days in the fridge, so feel free to make a little extra and enjoy with some more bread in that time.

METHOD

1. Blend together the **plant milk, tofu, brown sugar**, **maple syrup** and **cinnamon**

2. Pour the wet mixture into a wide shallow bowl

3. Soak both sides of each slice of **bread** in the wet mixture

4. Heat the **vegan butter** in a non-stick frying pan over medium-high heat

5. Once the butter is melted, fry the bread for a few minutes on each side until golden-brown

TO SERVE

6. Plate and top with a **knob of butter**, a dusting of **icing sugar** (through a sieve), the **banana** and the **maple syrup**

SEIZE THE SALAD VEGAN CAESAR

INGREDIENTS

2 vegan **chick'n fillets**

50g **breadcrumbs**

1 head romaine **lettuce**

½ tin drained **chickpeas**

30g **vegan parmesan**

FOR THE COATING

4 tbsp plain vegan **yogurt**

1 tsp **mustard**

1 tsp **agave syrup**

½ tsp **salt**

¼ tsp **pepper**

1 **garlic** clove

½ tsp **mixed herbs**

FOR THE DRESSING

2 tbsp **vegan mayonnaise**

2 tbsp **olive oil**

1 tbsp white wine **vinegar**

1 tsp **mustard**

1 tsp **agave syrup**

½ tsp **salt**

¼ tsp **pepper**

METHOD

1. Mix all **coating ingredients** in a bowl

2. Brush half the coating onto the **chick'n fillets** then cover with half of the **breadcrumbs**. Cook to packet instructions

3. Wash and roughly chop the **lettuce** and place in a large serving bowl

4. Cover the **chickpeas** with the other half of the coating and add to the lettuce

5. Once the fillets are cooked, add to the bowl (can first be chopped into bite-sized pieces)

6. Sprinkle on the **vegan parmesan** and the other half of the breadcrumbs

7. Make the dressing by shaking all the ingredients in a jar. Pour over the salad and toss everything together to serve

| Protein (g) | 23 | **30** |
| Calories (kcal) | 420 | mins |

Serves 2

FINER DETAIL

Chunks of tofu coated in cornflour and lightly fried can be substituted for the chick'n fillets.

Romaine is the classic choice for the salad, but - as seen in the photo - I often use up leftover spinach I have in the fridge, so feel able to use what you have.

BLACK FOREST SMOOTHIE BOWL

A thick cherry and chocolate smoothie you can scoop into a bowl with toppings galore

INGREDIENTS

FOR THE SMOOTHIE

250g frozen **cherries**

1 frozen **banana**

1 scoop (30g) chocolate flavoured **protein powder**

120ml **plant milk**

FOR THE TOPPINGS

1 **banana**

30g **walnuts**

20g homemade **granola**†

FINER DETAIL

Using frozen fruit and toppings like sliced banana and batch-baked granola helps keep this dish more affordable. Fresh cherries and cacao nibs would be a delicious but more expensive alternative.

If you only have plain or vanilla flavoured protein powder, add the same quantity but with an additional tsp of cocoa powder.

This smoothie is designed to be thick, to be eaten with a spoon. If you prefer it thinner, you can use fresh banana/add more plant milk.

I've found sweetened vegan oat milk works best with this recipe, but experiment to your heart's content.

† recipe on page 54

METHOD

1. To a blender, add the **smoothie ingredients** and blend until well combined. A strong blender should be able to do this in one go but, if weaker, pour the milk in slowly and add a little more than the recipe calls for if needed.

2. Pour the mixture into a bowl

3. Slice the **banana** into thin coins and roughly chop the **walnuts**

4. Gently place the banana slices on top of the smoothie, then sprinkle on the walnuts and **granola** ready to serve!

EGGLESS MAYO BAGUETTE

Protein (g)   12
Calories (kcal)   280

15 mins

Serves 2

INGREDIENTS

1 block **silken tofu** (300g), drained

1-2 **spring onions**

1 handful **rocket** (20g)

2 tbsp **vegan mayonnaise**

1 tsp **sriracha**

1 tsp **mustard**

1 tsp **black salt**

¼ tsp **black pepper**

Optionally ¼ tsp **turmeric**

1 tsp **nutritional yeast**

1 **baguette**

Butter to spread

METHOD

1. Remove **silken tofu** from its packet discarding the liquid. Cut into 1cm cubes and set aside

2. Peel and slice the **spring onions**

3. If using **rocket**, roughly chop so the leaves are more bite sized

4. In a large bowl combine the **mayonnaise, sriracha, mustard, black salt, black pepper** and the **turmeric** and **nutritional yeast**

5. Add the spring onions and rocket (set a little aside for a garnish, if you wish) and the tofu cubes

6. Gently stir to combine ingredients. Avoid over-stirring so the mixture does not become a paste

7. Cut your **baguette** into quarters and slice along the top partially through, then **butter**

8. Add the tofu mixture to the open baguettes, garnish with any remaining greens, salt and pepper

FINER DETAIL

If you don't fancy rocket, stick with classic cress.

Double the recipe and keep the mixture in the fridge to add to bread, salads or potato dishes throughout the week.

The black salt gives this its eggy taste, though you can use normal sea salt instead.

BLUEBERRY BLISS PANCAKES WITH HOMEMADE COMPOTE

INGREDIENTS

to make roughly 6 pancakes

FOR THE BATTER

1 **banana**

1 cup **sweet plant milk**

½ a tsp **vanilla extract**

1 cup **plain flour**

½ tsp **baking powder**

100g **fresh** or **frozen blueberries**

a little **oil** or **butter**

FOR THE BLUEBERRY COMPOTE

50g **fresh** or **frozen blueberries**

1 tbs **water**

1 tbsp **sugar**

1 tsp **lemon juice**

METHOD

FOR THE BATTER

1. Mash the **banana** in a large bowl
2. Slowly whisk in the **plant milk** and **vanilla extract**
3. Sift in the **flour** and **baking powder** and whisk to combine
4. Stir in the **blueberries**, leaving out a few to sprinkle on the top
5. Heat up a frying pan and add a little **oil** or **butter**.
6. Use one ladle of batter for each pancake, and cook evenly on both sides until slightly golden
7. Stack the pancakes, placing the freshest one at the bottom each time to keep them warm

FOR THE BLUEBERRY COMPOTE

8. Combine all the compote ingredients into a small saucepan
9. Cook on medium heat until the mixture simmers
10. Turn the heat down, and cook gently for another few minutes
11. Mash some of the blueberries with the back of a spoon to create a thicker texture while leaving some whole

FINER DETAIL

TO SERVE

Spoon the blueberry compote onto the pancake stack along with the extra blueberries you set aside earlier and a little extra sugar, syrup or agave

Make sure your banana is ripe for the right consistency.

It's important to gradually add the dry ingredients to the wet ingredients and not over whisk the batter mixture.

Additional toppings can include: vegan yogurt, other berries, syrups, and chopped nuts.

TEMPEH BUDDHA BOWL

Shredded tempeh paired with crunchy grated carrot and garlic roasted beetroot, all nestled on a bed of fluffy quinoa.

INGREDIENTS

FOR THE VEGETABLE TOPPINGS

2 **beetroots**

2 tsp **olive oil**

2 cloves **garlic**

2 **carrots**

FOR THE QUINOA BASE

180g **quinoa**

1 **stock cube**

360ml **boiling water**

FOR THE SHREDDED TEMPEH

2 tsp **olive oil**

200g **tempeh**

1 tsp **paprika**

1 tsp **onion powder**

1 tsp **soy sauce**

METHOD

FOR THE VEGETABLE TOPPINGS

1. Preheat the oven to 180°C
2. Wash then slice the **beetroot** thinly. Add the slices to a lined baking tray and drizzle with the **olive oil**
3. Peel the **garlic cloves** then thinly slice and place on top of the beetroot slices. Cook in the oven for 15-20 minutes
4. Grate the **carrots** and set aside for serving

FOR THE QUINOA BASE

5. Rinse the **quinoa** under cold water to remove any bitterness
6. Add a **stock cube** and the quinoa to the **boiling water** and cook to packet instructions
7. Once the quinoa is cooked, fluff it with a fork to separate the grains and set aside

FINER DETAIL

Optionally top with a handful of pine nuts or crispy onions for added texture.

The garlic slices will infuse their flavour into beetroot, so if you don't favour too strong of a garlic flavour, remove the slices after the beetroot is cooked and use in another recipe.

FOR THE SHREDDED TEMPEH

8. Heat the **oil** in a frying pan, then grate in the **tempeh** using a cheese grater

9. Stir for 3 minutes or so, then add in the **paprika**, **onion powder** and **soy sauce**. Cook for a further 5 minutes or until the tempeh reaches your desired level of crispiness

TO SERVE

10. Lastly, plate the quinoa, vegetable toppings and shredded tempeh with any sauce of your choice; I favour soy or sweet chilli

Nick's Homemade Granola

NICK'S HOMEMADE GRANOLA

My brother, who purchases pecans by the kilogram, has meticulously crafted this recipe and generously shares his delectable creations with the entire family.

INGREDIENTS

4 cups **oats**

3/4 cup **pecans**

3/4 cup whole **almonds**

a pinch of **salt**

1 tsp **ground cinnamon**

½ tsp **ground nutmeg**

½ cup **oil**

½ cup **maple syrup**

1 tsp **vanilla extract**

FINER DETAIL

Serve with plant milk or yogurt, with fruit and a little syrup or agave, or top on smoothie bowls (see page 44.)

Be mindful of timings with this recipe to avoid burning.

METHOD

1. Preheat the oven to 180°C

2. Combine the **oats**, **nuts**, **salt**, **cinnamon** and **nutmeg** in a large mixing bowl and stir together with a wooden spoon

3. Next, pour in the **oil**, **syrup** and **vanilla**. Mix well to combine the **wet and dry ingredients**

4. Spread the granola onto a lined baking tray. Compact the mixture then pat down with your spoon - this is key if you like your granola to cluster

5. Place the tray on the middle shelf of the oven and bake for 20 minutes. After the first 10 minutes, turn the tray round in the oven so each side cooks evenly.

6. Leave the granola to cool for at least 10 minutes before breaking into soft clusters and serving

PROTEIN WAFFLES

Sweet and satisfying, with four topping options, these protein waffles serve as an indulgent brunch or a treat to share! Makes 8 waffles.

INGREDIENTS

FOR THE BATTER

½ cup **plain flour**

1 tsp **baking powder**

1 scoop (30g) **protein powder**

1 cup sweetened **plant milk**

1 tbsp **maple syrup**

a dash of **oil** or a knob of **vegan butter**

FOR THE TOPPINGS

Classic: 2 tbsp of **vegan butter** with **maple syrup**

Biscoff: 75 g of **Biscoff spread** plus crushed **lotus biscuits**

Choc & Nut: 20g of chopped **hazelnuts** with **chocolate sauce**

Chocolate strawberry: Chocolate covered **strawberries** with a melted **chocolate** drizzle

METHOD

1. Grease the waffle iron with a spray of **oil** or using some baking paper to spread on **vegan butter**

2. Preheat the waffle iron

3. Stir the **dry ingredients** together in a bowl

4. Then whisk in the **milk** and **maple syrup** to create the batter

5. Ladle in the batter (a ladle should be enough for two waffles) and cook according to the appliance's instructions

6. Top your waffles with **spreads**, **sauces**, **chopped nuts** or **fruit** (or a combination of all of the above!) See posibilities below left

FINER DETAIL

I've intentionally not specified the protein powder flavour so you can tailor it to the toppings you choose. For example, I like pairing Speculoos protein powder with Biscoff toppings, or chocolate with chocolate covered strawberries, or plain vanilla with a little butter and maple syrup.

If you have a blender, feel able to blend all the ingredients to create a smoother batter.

SMASHED AVOCADO & SCRAMBLE BAGELS

INGREDIENTS

FOR THE SMASHED AVOCADO

1 ripe **avocado**

1 tbsp **nutritional yeast**

¼ tsp **garlic salt**

¼ tsp **black pepper**

A sprinkle of **chilli flakes**

FOR THE SCRAMBLE

Water for soaking (about 2 cups)

140g (1 cup) **pumpkin seeds**

120ml **water** (to blend)

1 tbsp **plant milk**

2 tbsp **nutritional yeast**

1 tsp **turmeric**

½ tsp **black salt**

¼ tsp **black pepper**

FOR SERVING

2 **bagels**

Vegan butter to spread

100g **cherry tomatoes**

METHOD

FOR THE SMASHED AVOCADO

1. Slice the **avocado** in half, pit it, then scoop out the flesh with a small cup or spoon

2. Smash the avocado with a fork until flattened, add the seasonings (**nutritional yeast**, **garlic salt**, **black pepper** and **chilli flakes**), and mix to your desired consistency

FOR THE PUMPKIN SEED SCRAMBLE

3. Bring a small pot of **water** (to soak) to the boil, then turn off the heat and add the **pumpkin seeds**. Leave to soak for an hour.

4. Drain the pumpkin seeds and add to a blender with the remaining **scramble ingredients** and blend until smooth

5. Pour the mixture in a non-stick pan and cook on medium heat until it bubbles

6. Move the mixture around as you would with a traditional scramble and cook to your chosen texture

Protein (g)	22	**20** mins
Calories (kcal)	477	

+ one hour to soak
Serves 2

TO SERVE

7. Halve and toast the **bagels**, then **butter**

8. Spread on the smashed avocado then top with the scramble

9. Slice the **cherry tomatoes** in half and add to the plate

10. Top with any of the seasonings you fancy, and enjoy!

FINER DETAIL

Black salt is what gives it an 'eggy taste' but can be replaced by sea salt.

If you like your scramble fluffy, mix in about half a tsp of baking powder after step 4.

The pumkin seed component can be replaced by tofu (silken or firm).

The scramble can be sealed and stored in the fridge for up to a week.

SOUPS AND SAUCES

ROASTED GARLIC AND TOMATO SOUP

INGREDIENTS

FOR THE ROASTING

½ head **garlic**

1 tbsp **olive oil**

2-3 large **tomatoes**

FOR THE SOUP

1 small **onion**

1 tbsp **olive oil**

1 tsp **salt**

¼ tsp **black pepper**

½ tsp **dried basil**

¼ tsp **dried thyme**

¼ tsp **chilli flakes**

2 cups **vegetable broth**

125ml **vegan single cream**

FINER DETAIL

Garlic bread is a lovely side for this dish. I like to buy ciabatta oven rolls then roast the full head of garlic and use half for the soup, and half for the garlic butter spread along with salt, pepper and a little parsley

METHOD

FOR THE ROASTING

1. Preheat your oven to 200°C and line a baking tray

2. Cut the very top off the half **garlic** head to expose the cloves, drizzle over the **oil,** wrap in some tin foil, and place on the baking tray

3. Halve the **tomatoes** and add to the tray. Roast the tomatoes and garlic for 20-25 minutes and allow to cool

FOR THE SOUP

4. Chop the **onion** and sauté in a medium saucepan with the **olive oil** until it starts to caramelise

5. Add the roasted tomatoes, **salt, black pepper, basil, thyme,** and **chilli flakes**

6. Add the garlic cloves by carefully squeezing out, using a paper towel. Stir well

7. Pour in the **vegetable broth** and simmer for about 10 minutes

8. Use an immersion blender to carefully blend the soup until it reaches your desired consistency

9. Stir in the **vegan single cream** and heat the soup, without boiling

10. Ladle the soup into serving bowls and drizzle with a little olive oil, cream and fresh herbs to taste

| Protein (g) | 6 | **40** |
| Calories (kcal) | 252 | mins |

Serves 2

CREAMY CHEESE SAUCE

INGREDIENTS

1 clove **garlic**

¼ cup unsweetened **plant milk**

60g **vegan cheddar**

150g **silken tofu**

1 tbsp **nutritional yeast**

1 tsp **lemon juice**

¼ tsp **dried basil**

¼ tsp **dried oregano**

¼ tsp **black pepper**

½ tsp **salt**

METHOD

1. Peel the **garlic** and place in a blender along with the **remaining ingredients**

2. Blend until smooth and creamy

FINER DETAIL

Silken tofu gives this sauce hidden protein and provides a creamy texture, but it's a base that can be replaced by soaked cashews or even blended cooked potatoes and carrots.

This sauce is used in my carbonara recipe, but it can also be used as a lower calorie and higher protein alternative for a roux.

MUM'S BABA GANOUSH

Protein (g)	3
Calories (kcal)	90

10 mins

+ 40 mintes roasting
Serves 2

This smoky and silky dip is dedicated to my mum and her unwavering commitment to preserving our planet. Thank you for all you do mum.

INGREDIENTS

1 **aubergine**

2 tbsp **olive oil** (1 for roasting, 1 for blending)

2 tbsp **lemon juice**

2 cloves **garlic** (peeled)

2 tbsp **tahini**

1 tsp **paprika**

1 tsp **salt**

FINER DETAIL

Serve with sliced bell pepper, carrot and cucumber, pita or even pizza crusts.

Store in the fridge for 3-5 days, and spread in your sandwiches throughout this time.

METHOD

1. Preheat oven to 180°C

2. Slice the **aubergine** in half, then score the face of each half into a diamond cross-hatch pattern going about half an inch deep

3. Place face up on a lined baking tray, and drizzle with 1 tbsp of the **olive oil**

4. Turn the aubergines over and roast the halves face down for about 40 minutes or until the aubergine is soft and the tops are golden brown

5. Let the aubergine cool before scooping out the flesh and adding to a blender or food processor

6. To the aubergine, add the **lemon juice**, **garlic**, **tahini**, **paprika**, **salt**, and the remaining tbsp of olive oil

7. Blend for less than a minute to keep some texture and serve

SOUPE AU PISTOU

INGREDIENTS

FOR THE SOUP

1 **small onion**

2 **garlic cloves**

100g **potatoes**

100g **green beans**

1 **carrot**

½ **courgette**

1 **tomato**

1 tbsp **olive oil**

4 cups **vegetable broth**

100g preferred **pasta**

½ tin **cannellini beans**

½ tsp **paprika**

½ tsp **salt**

¼ tsp black **pepper**

FOR THE PISTOU

50g fresh **basil**

30g **vegan parmesan**

50g **cashews**

2 **garlic cloves**

3 tbsp **olive oil**

2 tbsp **lemon juice**

METHOD

FOR THE SOUP

1. Roughly dice the **onion**, then peel and mince the **garlic cloves**

2. Cut the **potatoes** into small cubes, then top and tail and halve the **green beans**

3. Slice the **carrot** and **courgette** into coins, then dice the **tomato**

4. In a large pot, heat the **olive oil** over medium heat, then sauté the onions and garlic until translucent

5. Add the potato, green beans carrots and courgette to the pot. Sauté for a further 5 minutes

6. Add in the diced tomatoes, the **vegetable broth**, and the **pasta**. Cook on low-medium heat for 15 minutes, adding the **cannellini beans** with their juices for the last 5 minutes

7. Add the **paprika**, **salt** and **pepper,** and turn off the heat

FOR THE PISTOU

8. While the soup is cooking, prepare the pistou by blending all the ingredients together

| Protein (g) | 18 | **30** |
| Calories (kcal) | 473 | mins |

Serves 2

FINER DETAIL

Serve the soup and pistou separately, to allow each person to portion themselves.

If you intend to freeze the soup, I recommend omitting the pasta and adding freshly cooked pasta on the day of defrosting.

For the pistou, cashews can be replaced by pine nuts or walnuts.

Conchiglie pasta works well in this recipe.

DAD'S MIGHTY MINESTRONE SOUP

This meal, much like my father, is a timeless classic. Dad, thank you for the passing on the gift of cooking to me, and for the heart and warmth you bring to so many.

INGREDIENTS

1 **onion**

200g **potatoes** (maris piper is best)

1 **carrot**

2 **celery** stalks

50g **cavolo nero** or other dark cabbage

a dash of **oil**

2 **garlic** cloves (peeled)

½ cup tinned chopped **tomatoes** (with juice)

vegetable broth

180g preferred **pasta**

½ tsp **salt**

¼ tsp **black pepper**

dried herbs

200g (½ tin) **cannellini beans**

TO SERVE

30g grated **vegan cheese**

10g **fresh parsley**

a drizzle of **olive oil**

METHOD

1. Finely chop the **onion**; dice the **potatoes**, **carrots** and **celery**; and roughly chop the **cavolo nero**

2. Sauté the onion, potatoes, carrots, and celery with a little **oil** in a medium-sized pot. Mince the **garlic** and add to the pot for a further few minutes, stirring until fragrant

3. Pour in the **tomatoes**, **vegetable broth**, **pasta**, **salt**, **black pepper**, and **dried herbs**

4. Bring the soup to the boil and cook for 15-20 minutes, allowing the pasta and potatoes to cook through

5. Stir in the **cannellini beans** and cavolo nero and cook for 3 minutes, allowing the cavolo nero to wilt

TO SERVE

6. Turn the heat off and ladle into bowls. Top with the grated **vegan cheese**, **fresh pasley** and **olive oil**

FINER DETAIL

Making minestrone in bulk and freezing it often enhances its flavour - perfect for a lazy winter meal.

Punchy pesto (pg. 74) is also welcomed as a topping to this soup!

CREAMY HUMMUS WITH CRUNCHY CHICKPEAS

This delicious hummus dip is dedicated to my oldest friend, Alice - who was the first to tell me about veganism - and to her family who have always been so kind to me.

INGREDIENTS

FOR THE HUMMUS

1 tin **chickpeas** (including the liquid)

1 tbsp **tahini**

2 tbsp **lemon juice**

3 tbsp **olive oil**

3 **garlic cloves**, peeled

1 tsp **salt**

FOR THE CRUNCHY CHICKPEAS

1 tin **chickpeas** (drained)

a drizzle of **olive oil**

1 tsp **paprika**

½ tsp **salt**

FINER DETAIL

Hummus is best enjoyed with crudités or slathered into toasted pittas.

The crunchy chickpeas add extra protein and texture to the dip.

METHOD

1. Preheat the oven to 190°C

2. To a blender, add half the tin of **chickpeas** with all the liquid, **tahini**, **lemon juice**, **olive oil**, **garlic** and **salt**.

3. Blitz in a blender/processor until smooth then add the other half of the chickpeas, and blend for a shorter time so the mixture is just combined

4. Take the other drained tin and dry the **chickpeas** by rolling them between two kitchen towels. This should help to remove some of the skins too

5. Add the dried chickpeas to a baking tray with a drizzle of **olive oil** and the **paprika**

6. Cook for 15-20 minutes, then spoon on to the hummus with a sprinkle of **salt** and a little extra **paprika**

Protein (g)	6	Hummus	**5** mins	Crunchy Chickpeas	**20** mins
Calories (kcal)	190				

Serves 2

PUNCHY PESTO

INGREDIENTS

2 **garlic cloves**, peeled

3 tbsp **olive oil**

30g **vegan parmesan**

50g **fresh basil**

50g **cashews**

2 tbsp **lemon juice**

METHOD

1. Add **all the ingredients** to a blender, and blitz until well combined

2. Add a little more oil, if needed, for your desired consistency

FINER DETAIL

This recipe is used within others e.g. Soup au Pistou (page 66) and Pesto Pasta (pg. 76), but feel free to use it more broadly, to top soups, sandwiches and salads, for instance.

You can use pine nuts or walnuts instead of cashews.

I often use up any leftover spinach I have with this pesto, by adding it with a little more olive oil and lemon juice.

PASTA

PUNCHY PESTO AND GREEN BEAN PASTA

INGREDIENTS

FOR THE PESTO SAUCE

2 **garlic cloves**, peeled

3 tbsp **olive oil**

30g **vegan parmesan**

50g **fresh basil**

50g **cashews**

2 tbsp **lemon juice**

FOR THE PESTO PASTA

100g **fine green beans**

180g preferred **pasta**

1 packet vegan **lardons**

1 handful **pine nuts**

¼ cup **olives**

TO SERVE

Some grated **vegan cheese**

1 tsp **nutritional yeast**

a pinch of **pepper**

½ tsp **garlic salt**

FINER DETAIL

You can use pine nuts or walnuts instead of cashews.

METHOD

FOR THE PESTO SAUCE

1. Add **all the ingredients** to a blender, and blitz until well combined

2. Add a little more oil, if needed, for your desired consistency

FOR THE PESTO PASTA

3. Top and tail the **green beans**, and cut in half

4. Cook the **pasta** in salted boiling water to packet instructions, adding the green beans in the final five minutes

5. Fry the **lardons** in a frying pan and cook for a few minutes before adding the **pine nuts.** Cook until both are golden brown, and set aside

6. Drain the pasta and green beans, place back in the saucepan then stir in the **pesto**, lardons and pine nuts

7. Slice the **olives** in half and add

TO SERVE

8. Plate the pasta, grate on some **cheese**, and add **nutritional yeast, pepper** and **garlic salt**

Protein (g)	8	Pesto	**20**
Calories (kcal)	266	Pasta	mins
		Pesto	**10**
		Sauce	mins

Serves 2

79

SPAGHETTI CARBONARA

INGREDIENTS

80g **spaghetti**

½ tsp **salt**

60g **vegan lardons**

a dash of **oil**

FOR THE SAUCE

1 clove **garlic**

¼ cup unsweetened **plant milk**

60g **vegan cheddar**

150g **silken tofu**

1 tbsp **nutritional yeast**

1 tsp **lemon juice**

¼ tsp **dried basil**

¼ tsp **dried oregano**

¼ tsp **black pepper**

½ tsp **salt**

TO SERVE

10g **vegan parmesan**

10g **fresh parsley,** roughly chopped

1 tbsp **nutritional yeast**

½ tsp **garlic salt**

¼ tsp **black pepper**

METHOD

1. Cook the **spaghetti** until *al dente* in **salted water** according to packet instructions, drain but keep a little of the starchy water

2. Peel the **garlic** and place in a blender along with the remaining **sauce ingredients**

3. Blend until smooth and creamy

4. Fry the **vegan lardons** with a little **oil** in a large frying pan, following packet instructions (usually 5-7 minutes)

5. Add the spaghetti and the sauce to the frying pan and fold into one another. Add the starchy water here to thin the sauce if needed.

6. Once combined and heated, grate on the **parmesan** and top with the **fresh parsley**, **nutritional yeast**, **garlic salt** and **black pepper**

CHEESE AND TOMATO ORZO BAKE

INGREDIENTS

250g **orzo**

400ml **vegetable broth**

50g **vegan cheddar**

1 tbsp **nutritional yeast**

250g **cherry tomatoes**

½ tsp each of **garlic salt, pepper, dried basil** and **dried oregano**

METHOD

1. Preheat oven to 190°C

2. In a baking dish combine the **orzo** and **vegetable broth**

3. Grate the **vegan cheddar** on top, and sprinkle on the **nutritional yeast**

4. Slice the **tomatoes** in half and place on top of the cheese, seeded side facing upwards

5. Sprinkle over **all of the seasoning** (garlic salt, pepper, basil and oregano)

6. Cook for around 20 minutes, checking occasionally to see if a little more water is needed

7. Serve with your choice of greens, such as kale as shown here

SPAGHETTI AGLIO E OLIO

A garlicky Neapolitan dish you can make with cupboard ingredients in 15 minutes or less

INGREDIENTS

180g **spaghetti**

2 cloves **garlic**

2 tbsp **olive oil**

20g **pine nuts**

1 tsp **chilli flakes**

½ tsp **basil**

½ tsp **oregano**

1 tsp **salt**

1 tbsp **nutritional yeast**

FINER DETAIL

For extra indulgence and texture, add in about 50g of bread crumbs in step 4, and cook until golden.

For extra heat, use chilli oil instead of olive oil, and for less use only half a tsp of chilli flakes.

METHOD

1. Cook the **spaghetti** until *al dente* in salted water according to packet instructions, drain and set aside

2. Peel and mince the **garlic**

3. In a large frying pan, heat the **olive oil** and add the **pine nuts** for 1 minute on low heat, stirring often

4. Then add in the minced garlic and **chilli flakes** and cook until both the pine nuts and the garlic are golden brown

5. Turn off the heat and pour in the spaghetti

6. Toss together while adding the **basil**, **oregano**, **salt** and **nutritional yeast**. Add a little more oil here if needed

SPEEDY SPAGHETTI BOLOGNAISE

Protein (g)	44.7
Calories (kcal)	467

20 mins

+30 mins to rehydrate TVP mince
Serves 2

INGREDIENTS

60g **textured vegetable protein (TVP) mince**

30g **dried vegetable mix**

100ml **water**

250g **spaghetti**

1 small **onion**

1 tsp **celery**

a pinch of **salt**

2 tsp **paprika**

½ tsp **black pepper**

1 tbsp **nutritional yeast**

1 tin **chopped tomatoes**

TO SERVE

10g chopped **fresh parsley**

20g grated **vegan cheese**

10g **nutritional yeast**

Salt and **pepper**

FINER DETAIL

Using dried vegetables saves time, but freshly chopped are also fine.

Wholewheat pasta is used here

METHOD

1. In a bowl, combine the **TVP mince** and **dried vegetable mix**. Add the **water** to the bowl and let it sit for about 30 minutes to rehydrate (but refer to packet instructions)

2. Meanwhile, bring a pot of salted water to a boil, add the **spaghetti** and cook until *al dente*. Once cooked, drain the spaghetti and set it aside

3. Roughly chop the **onion** and sauté with a little oil, in a frying plan, for 2-3 minutes until translucent

4. Add the mince and vegetables to the pan, along with the **celery salt**, **paprika**, **black pepper**, and **nutritional yeast**. Stir well to combine, and let it cook for another 5 minutes

5. Next, pour in the **chopped tomatoes** and bring the mixture to a gentle simmer. Cover the pan, and let it cook for 10 minutes to allow the sauce to thicken

TO SERVE

6. Plate the cooked spaghetti and ladle in the bolognese sauce over the spaghetti. Garnish with the **fresh parsley**, grated **vegan cheese**, **nutritional yeast**, **salt** and **pepper**, if desired.

TOM'S CREAMY GARLIC AND CHICK'N SPAGHETTI

Tom taught me this recipe and it's one he often cooks for me, so is a cherished favourite. They may speak of only five love languages, but evidently, pasta was overlooked.

INGREDIENTS

180g **spaghetti**

80g vegan **chick'n pieces**

1 tbsp **olive oil**

1 tbsp **vegan butter**

3 cloves **garlic**

½ cup unsweetened **soy milk**

25g **vegan cheese**

½ tsp **garlic salt**

¼ tsp **black pepper**

FINER DETAIL

Use a microplane grater for the garlic and vegan cheese for a finer sauce.

Serve with fresh parsley, more grated cheese and a little salt and pepper.

METHOD

1. Bring a saucepan of salted water to the boil, add the **spaghetti** and cook until *al dente* according to packet instructions. Drain the spaghetti, keeping a little of the water to add to the sauce later, and set aside

2. Meanwhile, fry the **chick'n pieces** in a little oil until golden brown and crispy. Set the chick'n aside

3. In the same frying pan, now pour the tbsp of **olive oil** into the centre of the pan on low-medium heat. Next, spoon in the **vegan butter** to melt

4. Peel and mince the **garlic** and add to the frying pan, cooking until golden

5. Next, lower the heat and whisk in the **soy milk**. Then slowly grate in the **vegan cheese** and whisk again to combine. Cook until the vegan cheese has melted and the sauce heats up. If you prefer it thinner, you can add in the water set aside earlier here

6. Lastly, combine all the components together (the spaghetti, the sauce, and the chick'n) in the pan and cook on low heat until hot. Stir in the **garlic salt** and **black pepper** and serve

CHEESY BROCCOLI BAKE

INGREDIENTS

FOR THE BROCCOLI BAKE

½ head **broccoli**

180g preferred **pasta**

FOR THE ROUX

2 tbsp **vegan butter**

2 tbsp **plain flour**

1 cup unsweetened **soy milk**

¼ cup **vegan cheddar cheese**

¼ tsp **dried oregano**

½ tsp **salt**

¼ tsp **black pepper**

TO TOP BEFORE BAKING

½ cup **grated vegan cheddar** cheese

2 tbsp **nutritional yeast**

½ tsp **garlic salt**

METHOD

FOR THE BROCCOLI BAKE

1. Preheat your oven to 190°C
2. Cut the **broccoli** into small florets
3. Cook the **pasta** until *al dente*, adding the broccoli for the final 3-4 minutes
4. Drain the pasta and broccoli. You can optionally rinse the broccoli in cold water to stop it cooking further
5. Add the pasta and broccoli to a large oven-proof dish and set aside

FOR THE ROUX

6. In a small saucepan, melt the **vegan butter** over medium heat
7. Whisk in the **flour** for a couple of minutes to form a paste
8. Gradually whisk in the **soy milk** until the sauce is smooth and thick
9. Grate in the **vegan cheese** and cook until it's melted in, then stir in the **oregano**, **salt** and **pepper**
10. Pour the roux into the oven-proof dish with the pasta and broccoli
11. Sprinkle the **grated cheese**, **nutritional yeast** and **garlic salt** over the dish and bake for 20 minutes, or until the top is golden brown and the sauce is bubbling

| Protein (g) | 15 | **20** |
| Calories (kcal) | 315 | mins |

+ 20 minutes baking
Serves 2

FINER DETAIL

You can mix in breadcrumbs with the grated cheese topping to add extra texture.

For pasta, I enjoy conchiglie as its shell shape means it can hold sauce. Any pasta will work but consider the cooking time needed for the broccoli.

COURGETTE AND LEMON TAGLIATELLE

INGREDIENTS

180g **tagliatelle**

½ **courgette**

3 tbsp **olive oil**

The juice of half a **lemon**

2 tsp **nutritional yeast**

1 tsp **garlic salt**

¼ tsp **black pepper**

25g **pistachios**, roughly chopped

1 tbsp chopped **chives**

FINER DETAIL

The courgette can also be pan-fried in a non-stick pan without oil to save on calories

To add a kick, use chilli oil instead of olive oil Mix and match with your favourite type of pasta, or even try the courgette and dressing with a salad

METHOD

1. Preheat the oven to 180°C

2. Cook the **tagliatelle** until *al dente* in salted water according to packet instructions

3. While the tagliatelle cooks, thinly slice the **courgette** and spread onto a lined baking tray with 1 tbsp of **olive oil**. Grill for 8-10 minutes at 180°C

4. Drain the tagliatelli, and place it in a serving bowl keeping a little of the starchy water in the pot

5. Stir in the remaining 2 tbsp of olive oil, along with the **lemon juice**, **nutritional yeast**, **garlic salt**, and **black pepper**

6. Add the courgette and **pistachios**

7. Top with the chopped **chives**, a drizzle of olive oil and any of the seasoning if desired

ROASTED RED PEPPER PASTA

INGREDIENTS

180g preferred **pasta**

20g **pine nuts**

80g **kalamata olives**

1 tbsp **nutritional yeast**

½ tsp **chilli flakes**

FOR THE SAUCE

1/3 cup unsweetened **oat milk**

150g **roasted red peppers** (from a jar)

30g **vegan cheese** (cheddar or parmesan)

150g **silken tofu**

2 cloves **garlic**

1 tbsp **nutritional yeast**

1 tsp **salt**

¼ tsp **black pepper**

METHOD

1. Cook the **pasta** until *al dente* in salted water according to packet instructions, drain and set aside

2. Make the sauce by blending all the **sauce ingredients** in a blender or food processor until creamy. Add a little more **milk** for a thinner sauce

3. Dry fry the **pine nuts** in a frying pan. Be careful that they don't burn

4. Pit the **olives** and slice into halves

5. Pour the sauce and pasta into the saucepan that cooked the pasta, and combine on low heat until hot

6. Stir in the pine nuts, olives, **nutritional yeast** and **chilli flakes** and serve

FINER DETAIL

Optionally top with your choice of grated vegan cheese.

If you only have fresh peppers, you can roast them yourself in a lined baking tray at 200°C for 30 minutes, or until the skin is slightly blistered.

To meal prep for the next day, make double the sauce and only blend the peppers in one half, saving the other half for a carbonara.

MEDITERRANEAN PINK PASTA

INGREDIENTS

FOR THE MEDITERRANEAN VEGETABLES

½ **courgette**

250g **cherry tomatoes**

100g **asparagus**

a dash of **oil**

½ tsp **salt**

½ tsp **dried rosemary**

FOR THE PASTA AND PINK SAUCE

180g preferred **pasta**

a dash of **oil**

2 cloves **garlic**, minced

1 tsp **chilli flakes**

2 tbsp **passata**

250ml **soya cream**

1.2 tsp **salt**

½ tsp **black pepper**

TO SERVE

a drizzle of **oil**

dried rosemary

a little **vegan grated cheese**

METHOD

FOR THE MEDITERRANEAN VEGETABLES

1. Preheat the oven to 180°C
2. Cut the **courgette** vertically in half then slice horizontally into thin semicircles
3. Halve the **tomatoes**
4. Cut off the **asparagus** ends, then cut the stems into bite-sized pieces
5. Add all the vegetables to a lined baking tray with a little **oil**, the **salt** and **dried rosemary**
6. Cook for 15 minutes or until slightly browned, flipping the vegetables over at the half-way mark

FINER DETAIL

Optionally top with fresh basil and cracked black pepper.

You could steam the courgette and asparagus or stir-fry all of the vegetables.

Swap out olive oil for chilli oil for an extra kick.

FOR THE PASTA AND PINK SAUCE

7. Cook the **pasta** until *al dente* in salted water according to packet instructions, drain and set aside

8. In a separate saucepan, add a little **oil** and heat with the minced **garlic** and **chilli flakes**

9. Once the garlic is slightly golden, add the **passata**

10. After a few minutes, stir in the **cream**, **salt** and **pepper** to create the pink sauce

11. Leave to simmer for 2-3 minutes, then pour the sauce over the pasta and add the vegetables

TO SERVE

12. Top with a drizzle of **oil**, **dried rosemary** and a little **vegan grated cheese** if you care for it

RICE

THE ULTIMATE SUSHI BOWL

INGREDIENTS

FOR THE IMITATION TUNA

2 large **tomatoes**

2 cloves **minced garlic**

1 tsp **minced or powdered ginger**

1 tbsp **sesame oil**

1 tbsp **maple syrup**

¼ cup **soy sauce**

FOR THE SUSHI BOWL

2 cups **sushi rice**

1 **avocado**

½ **cucumber**

80g **vegan chick'n**

1 tbsp **sesame oil**

1 tbsp **vegan mayonnaise**

1 tbsp **sriracha**

2 tbsp **hoisin**

METHOD

FOR THE IMITATION TUNA

1. Score the **tomatoes** and submerge in boiling water

2. Remove the tomatoes when the skin starts to split. Place in cold water

3. Peel off the skin and cut into four. Deseed the tomatoes. Cut into strips

4. Combine the **other imitation tuna ingredients** in a bowl, to make the marinade

5. Add the strips to the marinade and leave for at least two hours (ideally overnight)

FOR THE SUSHI BOWL

6. Cook **sushi rice** following packet instructions, and cover

7. Slice the **avocado**, **cucumber** and any other fresh vegetables of choice

8. Fry the **chick'n** with **sesame oil** in a pan until golden brown

9. Turn the heat down and add the imitation tuna marinade to glaze the chick'n, leaving the tomatoes in the bowl. Stir well.

10. Mix the **mayo** and **sriracha** in a separate bowl for the sauce

11. Plate the rice, then the fresh veg, chick'n, marinade, imitation tuna, and add **hoisin** and sriracha mayo

Protein (g)	20	Imitation Tuna	**20** mins	Sushi Bowl	**25** mins
Calories (kcal)	755				

marinade for a minimum of two hours
Serves 2

FINER DETAIL

Other optional toppings:
- toasted sesame seeds
- diced spring onions
- shredded carrot
- nori seaweed strips
- pickled ginger
- wasabi paste

BUTTER TOFU CURRY

INGREDIENTS

2 cups **basmati rice**

1 **onion**

3 tbsp **vegan butter**

2 cloves **garlic**

1 tsp **cumin**

1 tsp **turmeric**

1 tsp **garam masala**

250ml **passata**

200g **firm tofu**

200ml **coconut milk**

2 tbsp **vegetable oil**

10g **fresh coriander**

FINER DETAIL

Serve with naan, paratha, chapati, or puri.

The photo shows butter beans in place of tofu as a cheaper and quicker alternative. If using butter beans, just skip step 7 and 8 and add the beans in step 9.

You can replace the coconut milk with vegan soya, oat or cashew cream, to make a slightly thicker curry.

METHOD

1. Cook **rice** to packet instructions

2. Start the butter sauce by dicing the **onion** and softening in 2 tbsps **vegan butter** in a frying pan on medium heat

3. Peel and mince the **garlic**

4. Once the onion is translucent, add the garlic, **cumin**, **tumeric** and **garam masala** to the pan and sauté for a few minutes until fragrant

5. Pour in the **passata** and cook for 5 minutes

6. Turn the heat down, pour in the **coconut milk**, then let simmer for 5 minutes

7. Tear the **tofu** into small cubes and thoroughly coat in the **cornflour**

8. Fry the tofu pieces in a separate pan with a little **vegetable oil** until golden brown

9. Add the tofu pieces and the remaining vegan butter to the curry sauce, stirring to combine. Simmer for 2 minutes

10. Take off the heat and serve the curry on top of the rice, with a little extra butter and **coriander** if you like

MIA'S GENERAL TSO TOFU

Mia, you're this recipe's biggest fan and with golden tofu, sugar and spice, I don't blame you. Here's to more daydreaming and late night talking from the dining table - with me in your seat ;))

INGREDIENTS

2 cups **sushi rice**

200g firm **tofu**

2-3 tbsp **cornflour**

1 tbsp **sesame oil**

2 cloves minced **garlic**

1 inch piece **ginger**, peeled and minced

FOR THE SAUCE

¼ cup **soy sauce**

½ tsp **chilli flakes**

1 tbsp **brown sugar**

1 tbsp **rice vinegar**

1 tbsp **sesame oil**

FINER DETAIL

Optional toppings include: white sesame seeds, sliced spring onions, a drizzle of hoisin, and vegetables of choice.

The sugar can be replaced by maple syrup, agave syrup or even a splash of orange or pineapple juice.

METHOD

1. Cook the **rice** to packet instructions

2. Tear the **tofu** into small cubes and thoroughly coat in the **cornflour**

3. Fry the tofu on medium heat in the **sesame oil** until light brown in colour

4. Turn the heat to low, and add the **garlic** and **ginger** to the frying pan for a few minutes, as the tofu crispens

FOR THE SAUCE

5. Combine the **sauce ingredients** in a small bowl and pour into the pan, coating the tofu. Cook for a few minutes, or until caramelised

TO SERVE

6. Serve on a bed of rice with the optional garnishes and vegetables of choice

RED THAI CURRY

INGREDIENTS

2 cups **rice**

½ **onion**

200g **baby potatoes** (about 6)

100g **broccoli**

1 **carrot**

200ml **coconut milk** (half tin)

200g **chickpeas** (half tin)

75g **mangetout**

80g vegan **chick'n** pieces

FOR THE CURRY PASTE

½ **onion**

3 red thai **chilli peppers**

1 inch piece **ginger**

2 cloves **garlic**

1 tsp ground **coriander**

½ tsp **paprika**

½ tsp **salt**

¼ tsp **black pepper**

2 tbsp **soy sauce**

1 tbsp **lime juice**

1 tsp **agave syrup**

METHOD

1. Cook **rice** to packet instructions and set aside

2. Next, prep the curry paste: Roughly chop half the **onion**, cut the ends off the **chilli peppers**, and peel the **ginger**

3. Place all the **paste ingredients** into a blender or food processor and blitz until you have a smooth paste

4. For the curry: Dice the other half of the **onion** and soften in a little oil in a sauté pan on medium heat. Stir in the paste then turn off the heat

5. Quarter the **baby potatoes**, cut the **broccoli** into bite-sized pieces, and peel and slice the **carrot**

6. Add all the vegetables to the pan and stir to allow the paste mixture to coat the vegetables, on a low-medium heat

7. Pour in the **coconut milk** and cook for 10-15 minutes with a lid to cook the vegetables. Add in the **chickpeas** and the **mangetout** for the final 5 mins

8. Meanwhile, fry the **chick'n** pieces with a little oil until golden and crispy in a second frying pan

9. Add the chick'n to the sauté pan, mix in, then serve over rice.

| Protein (g) | 24 | **40** |
| Calories (kcal) | 530 | mins |

Serves 2

FINER DETAIL

Baby corn or tinned sweetcorn is also a lovely addition. Feel free to use any veg that might otherwise go to waste at the bottom of your fridge.

Using a jar of pre-made curry paste can save you time.

KUNG PAO

INGREDIENTS

FOR THE SAUCE

120ml (½ cup) **vegetable broth**

2 tbsp **soy sauce**

1 tbsp **rice vinegar**

1 tbsp **hoisin sauce**

1 tbsp **maple syrup**

1 tsp **cornflour**

FOR THE STIR-FRY

2 tbsps **vegetable oil**

80g **vegan chick'n**

1 white **onion**

2 bell **peppers** (one red, one yellow)

1 red **chilli pepper**

3 cloves **garlic**, peeled

1 cm cube **ginger**

½ cup **dry roasted peanuts**

TO SERVE

1 cup (250g) **sushi rice**

10g **fresh coriander**

2-3 **spring onions**

A handful of **dry roasted peanuts**

108

METHOD

1. Cook **rice** to packet instructions

FOR THE SAUCE

2. In a small bowl or jug, combine all the **wet sauce ingredients**

3. Whisk in the **cornflour** and set aside

FOR THE STIR-FRY

4. Heat half the **oil** in a wok or large pan over medium-high heat

5. Add the vegan **chick'n** pieces and fry until golden brown and crispy. Remove the chick'n and set aside

6. Dice the **onion** and **peppers** (red, yellow and **chilli**). Mince the **garlic** and **ginger**

7. To the pan, add the remaining oil and the chilli peppers and fry until fragrant (1 minute)

8. Add the onion and fry until translucent, before adding the minced garlic and ginger. Stir-fry for another 1-2 minutes

9. Stir in the diced bell peppers and fry until they start to soften

10. Add the chick'n back into the wok, along with the **dry roasted peanuts**

11. Once combined, pour in the sauce to coat the mixture. Leave for a few minutes to allow the sauce to thicken, then remove from the heat

TO SERVE

12. Serve over cooked rice, and garnish with **fresh coriander**, chopped **spring onion** and a handful of dry roasted **peanuts**

FINER DETAIL

Try tamari sauce for a gluten-free alternative to soy sauce.

Tofu coated in cornflour works really nicely as a substitute for the chick'n.

Add green pepper if you actually like it...

NASI GORENG

INGREDIENTS

2 cups **basmati rice**

1 white/brown **onion**

½ **cabbage**

3 cloves **garlic**, peeled

1 **carrot**

150g **silken tofu**

2 tbsp **soy sauce**

1 tbsp **maple syrup**

Juice of half a **lime**

¼ tsp **chilli flakes**

A handful of **fresh coriander**

FINER DETAIL

My dad used to make a very similar recipe for my family with a fried egg on top. I've found mixing in some silken tofu to work for me, but you could also pan fry thin strips of firm tofu with a little oil and black salt.

Leftovers will last 3-4 days in the fridge or 2-3 months in the freezer in an air-tight container.

METHOD

1. Cook the **rice** to packet instructions

2. Thinly slice the **onion** and **cabbage** into bite sized strips, then mince the **garlic**

3. Peel then grate the **carrot**

4. Heat up the oil in a large frying pan or wok, then add the onion and stir until translucent. Lower the heat and cook the garlic for 2 minutes

5. Add the sliced cabbage and grated carrot and fry on medium heat until everything has softened and is golden brown

6. Next, squeeze in the **silken tofu** as is, and stir into the vegetables until well combined

7. Add in the cooked rice and stir to combine

8. Lower the heat and add the **soy sauce**, **maple syrup**, **lime juice** and **chilli flakes**. Cook for a further 5 minutes

9. Plate into bowls and top with the fresh **coriander** and a dash of soy sauce

Protein (g)   23.7
Calories (kcal)   455

30
mins

JOLLOF RICE AND FRIED OYSTER MUSHROOM

Jollof, a fragrant, tomato-infused rice dish with a delightful kick, pairs harmoniously with the incredibly meaty texture of fried oyster mushrooms. Served with hot sauce, these components unite to make a fiery feast.

INGREDIENTS

FOR THE JOLLOF

1 **onion**

4 **garlic** cloves, peeled

3 tbsp **vegetable oil**

100 ml **tomato purée**

1 **vegan stock cube**

2 cups **boiling water**

200g (½ tin) **chopped tomatoes**

2 1/3 cups **basmati rice**

FOR THE SPICES

1 tsp **scotch bonnet chilli powder**

1 tsp **ground ginger**

1 tsp **curry powder**

1 tsp **fennel seeds**

1 tsp **cayenne pepper**

FOR THE BATTER

70g **plain flour**

½ cup **soy milk**

1 tsp **mustard**

1 tsp **salt**

½ tsp **garlic powder**

½ tsp **onion powder**

¼ tsp **paprika**

FOR THE FRIED OYSTER MUSHROOMS

150g **oyster mushrooms**

¼ cup **vegetable oil**

FINER DETAIL

Serve with hot sauce and a sprinkle of salt.

Fry the mushroom in batches if needed, so as to not overcrowd the pan.

METHOD

FOR THE JOLLOF AND SPICES

1. Finely chop the **onion** and mince the **garlic**

2. In a large pot, sauté the onion in the **vegetable oil** on low heat until translucent, then add the garlic for a minute or two, stirring well

3. Add in the **tomato purée** and **the spices** and cook for a further 5 minutes until thick and fragrant

4. Create a stock with the **stock cube** and **boiling water**. Add to the pot, with the **chopped tomatoes**

5. Rinse the **rice**, add to the pot, and bring to the boil. Then, reduce the heat to low, cover with a lid and cook for 40 minutes (without lifting the lid)

FOR THE BATTER

6. Whisk together the **batter ingredients** in a large mixing bowl

FOR THE FRIED OYSTER MUSHROOMS

7. Cut the **mushrooms** into smaller pieces

8. Heat the **vegetable oil** for frying

9. Dip each mushroom piece into the batter with two forks, then carefully place into the oil and fry for 2-3 minutes on each side until golden brown

10. Remove the battered mushrooms with a slotted spoon and place them on a paper towel-lined plate to drain the excess oil

11. Plate all components while hot

113

ALOO KI BHUJIA

Simple and cheap as chips, this is a tomato-based curry with golden potatoes. Serve with rice and/or my tomato and spinach dahl recipe (page 116)

INGREDIENTS

2 cups **basmati rice**

1 **onion**

3 **garlic cloves**

500g **potatoes**

2 tbsp **vegetable oil**

1 tsp **cumin seeds**

1 tsp **garam masala**

1 tsp **ground turmeric**

½ tsp **chilli powder**

1 tsp **salt**

200g (½ tin) **chopped tomatoes**

OPTIONAL SIDES AND TOPPINGS

Puri, **chapati**, **roti**, **paratha** or **naan**

A handful of **fresh dill**

A squeeze of **lemon juice**

FINER DETAIL

You can parboil the potatoes for a faster cooking time overall.

METHOD

1. Cook **rice** to packet instructions
2. Finely dice the **onion**, then peel and mince the **garlic cloves**
3. Roughly dice the **potatoes** into bite-sized pieces
4. Heat the **vegetable oil** in a large frying pan with the **cumin seeds**
5. Once it starts to splutter, add the onion and cook until transparent, before adding the garlic for a further few minutes. Stir well
6. Now add the **garam masala**, **turmeric**, **chilli powder** and **salt**.
7. Stir in the potatoes to coat them in the spices
8. Fry the potatoes for 10 minutes, letting them crispen. Add more oil if needed
9. Add the **chopped tomatoes**, and cook on low heat for a further 10-15 minutes. Stir to prevent sticking
10. Remove from the heat once the tomatoes have reduced and the potatoes are fully cooked
11. Serve with the rice and optional sides and toppings

TOMATO AND SPINACH DAHL

INGREDIENTS

2 cups **basmati rice**

FOR THE DHAL

½ cup **red lentils**

1½ cups **water**

1 tsp **turmeric**

1 tsp **salt**

½ tsp **cumin**

½ tsp **ground coriander**

½ tsp **garam masala**

½ tsp **mustard seeds**

1 white **onion**

2 cloves **garlic**, peeled

1-inch piece fresh **ginger**

1 tbsp **coconut oil**

200g (½ tin) **chopped tomatoes**

1 cup **fresh spinach**

Juice of half a **lemon**

2 tbsp **vegan cream**

TO SERVE

Fresh **chives**, chopped

Lemon wedges

METHOD

1. Cook **rice** to packet instructions

2. Rinse the **lentils** under cold water until the water runs clear

3. In a saucepan, combine the rinsed lentils, **water**, **turmeric**, **salt**, **cumin**, **coriander**, **garam masala**, and **mustard seeds**, and bring the mixture to the boil

4. Reduce the heat to low, cover, and simmer for 15-20 minutes

5. Meanwhile, dice the **onion**, mince the **garlic**, and peel and finely chop the **ginger**

6. Heat the **coconut oil** in a large frying pan over medium heat and sauté the onion until it becomes translucent

7. Add the garlic and ginger to the frying pan and stir for 1-2 minutes until fragrant

8. Add the chopped **tomatoes** and simmer for 5 minutes to thicken

9. Roughly chop the spinach then stir in and cook for another few minutes until the spinach wilts, then pour in the **lemon juice**

10. Add the lentils and **vegan cream** to the frying pan and stir to combine

11. Serve with the **chives** and **lemon**

FINER DETAIL

Serve with cooked rice, fresh coriander and lemon wedges.

Taste and adjust the seasoning to your preference, with more salt, spice, or lemon juice.

If you have fresh tomatoes, dice 2-3 as a substitute for the tinned tomatoes.

JOLENE'S LOUISIANA GUMBO

INGREDIENTS

2 cups **basmati rice**

1 **white onion**

1 green **bell pepper**

1 yellow **bell pepper**

2 **celery stalks**

1 cup **okra**

6 **vegan sausages**

2 tbsp **vegan butter**

2 tbsp all-purpose **flour**

2 cloves **garlic**, minced

2 cups **vegetable broth**

200g (½ tin) **chopped tomatoes**, undrained

1 tsp **paprika**

½ tsp **oregano**

¼ tsp **cayenne pepper**

1 tsp **salt**

½ tsp **black pepper**

2-3 **spring onions**

METHOD

1. Cook the **rice** to packet instructions and put aside

2. Dice the **white onion**, **bell peppers**, **celery** and **okra**

3. Cook the **sausages** to packet instructions (grill or fry). Once cool, cut into bite-size pieces

4. To create the roux, in a large pot, melt the **butter** over medium heat, then add the **flour** and whisk until deep brown in colour

5. Add the diced vegetables and **garlic** to the pot and stir to coat in the roux, cooking for 5 minutes until the vegetables are softened

6. Pour in the **vegetable broth** and **chopped tomatoes**, along with the **paprika**, **oregano**, **cayenne pepper**, **salt**, and **black pepper**. Stir to combine and simmer for 20 minutes

7. Add the sliced vegan sausage for a final 2 minutes in the pot

8. Serve the gumbo over the cooked rice, and garnish with the chopped **spring onions**

| Protein (g) | 30 | **50** |
| Calories (kcal) | 560 | mins |

Serves 2

FINER DETAIL

Okra can be fresh or frozen.

To adjust the spice of the dish, adjust the quantity of cayenne pepper.

This gumbo can be made ahead and can even taste better with time! Refrigerate in an airtight container for up to 5 days.

NOODLES

CRISPY TOFU RAMEN

INGREDIENTS

½ head **broccoli**

100g (2 nests) **ramen** or **rice noodles**

200g firm **tofu**

3 tbsp **cornflour**

1 tsp **sesame oil**

2 **spring onions**, chopped

1 tsp **sesame seeds**

1 tbsp **hoisin** sauce

FOR THE BROTH

1 vegan chick'n **stock cube**

1 tsp **garlic powder** or paste

1 tsp **onion powder**

½ tsp **ground cumin**

½ tsp **ground ginger**

1 tsp **sesame oil**

2 tbsp **soy sauce**

METHOD

1. Slice the **broccoli** into small florets

2. Add the **ramen** to a pot of boiling water

3. Crumble in the **stock cube**, and stir in all the remaining **broth ingredients**

4. Cook the ramen to packet instructions, allowing the broth ingredients to be absorbed into the noodles. Add the broccoli for the last 3-4 minutes of cooking, then take off the heat

5. Tear the **tofu** into small cubes and thoroughly coat in the **cornflour**

6. Fry the tofu on medium heat in the **sesame oil** until golden brown and crispy

7. Ladle in the noodles, broccoli and broth into deep bowls. Top with the crispy tofu, chopped **spring onions, sesame seeds** and a drizzle of **hoisin**

FINER DETAIL

The broccoli can also be cooked in a wok with other vegetables like pak choi, carrots and beansprouts and/or of course whatever you have.

I use OXO Meat-Free Chicken flavour stock, but you can use vegetable stock.

Wok and Roll Sticky 'Duck' Stir Fry

WOK AND ROLL STICKY 'DUCK' STIR FRY

INGREDIENTS

2 nests **noodles**

½ head **cabbage**

4 **spring onions**

2 cloves **garlic**

1 tbsp **sesame oil**

100g shredded **vegan duck**

100g frozen **peas**

2 tbsp **soy sauce**

1 tsp **brown sugar**

2 tbsp **hoisin sauce**

1 tsp **sriracha**

1 tsp **sesame seeds**

FINER DETAIL

The cabbage may initially look daunting in the wok, but it bulks out the meal for a lower calorie but high density dish.

For crispier vegan duck, fry in a separate frying pan and add nearer to the end.

Serve with Kimchi, for spice and an extra crunch.

METHOD

1. Cook the **noodles** to packet instructions and set aside

2. Thinly slice the **cabbage**, cutting it in half, then into long slices

3. Slice the **spring onions** and separate the white and green slices

4. Peel and mince the **garlic** cloves

5. Pour the **sesame oil** into a wok, adding in the minced garlic when the oil is hot

6. After a minute, add in the cabbage and white slices of the spring onion and wok-fry on high heat for 10 minutes, stirring often

7. Once the cabbage and spring onion have softened with flecks of brown, add in the **vegan duck**

8. Wok-fry for another 5 minutes before adding the frozen **peas**, **soy sauce**, **brown sugar**, **hoisin**, and **sriracha**. Cook for 2-3 minutes

9. Add the cooked noodles to the wok and stir to combine

10. Serve with the remaining green slices of the spring onions, the **sesame seeds** and a drizzle of hoisin

Vietnamese Noodle Bowl

VIETNAMESE NOODLE BOWL

INGREDIENTS

FOR RICE PAPER ROLLS

200g firm **tofu**

½ a red **bell pepper**

1 **carrot**

1 **cucumber**

½ head **romaine lettuce**

8 **rice paper wrappers**

50g **mint leaves**

20g **dry roasted peanuts**

100g (2 nests) **thin rice noodles**

FOR THE PEANUT SAUCE

2 tbsp **peanut butter**

2 tbsp **soy sauce**

1 tbsp **sesame oil**

1 tbsp **lime juice**

1 tbsp **brown sugar**

1 clove **garlic**, minced

½ tsp ground **ginger**

FOR THE NOODLE BOWL BASE

Any remaining julienned vegetables, noodles, peanuts and mint leaves

METHOD

FOR RICE PAPER ROLLS

1. Cook noodles to packet instructions

2. Cut the **tofu** into thin strips and pan fry with a drizzle of oil until golden brown and crispy

3. Follow steps 3 to 6 for each roll. Julienne or shred the **pepper**, **carrot** and **cucumber**, and roughly chop the **romaine lettuce**

4. Fill a shallow bowl with warm water and submerge each **rice paper wrapper** for 10 seconds or until pliable

5. Transfer to a plate and layer on to the centre bottom of each wrapper: romaine lettuce, **mint leaves**, julienned pepper, carrot and cucumber, tofu strips, **dry roasted peanuts** and cooked **noodles**

6. Gently fold over left and right of each wrapper inwards, then roll up the wrapper tightly from the bottom until sealed. Use a little water on your finger to fully close the seam

7. Slice each roll in half diagonally, ready to serve

FOR THE PEANUT DIPPING SAUCE

8. In a bowl, whisk **all the sauce ingredients** together until well combined. Adjust to your liking

FOR THE NOODLE BOWL BASE

9. Place the halved rolls in the centre of a plate, surrounded by any remaining filling ingredients

10. Dip in the peanut sauce before devouring!

FINER DETAIL

Vermicelli noodles work well, and romaine lettuce can be replaced by napa cabbage.

The folding process is similar to making a burrito but I advise watching a video to master it.

To enhance the recipe further, make a half more of the peanut sauce and use the extra quantity to coat the tofu strips before frying.

If you have a nut allergy, sweet chilli sauce works well instead.

SIMON'S SWEET POTATO LAKSA

To my brother, who worked extensively with me on this book, and who absolutely demolishes this dish. Thank you.

INGREDIENTS

FOR THE LAKSA PASTE

½ **onion**

1 clove **garlic**

A thumb-sized piece peeled **ginger**

1 red **chilli pepper**

½ tsp **turmeric**

½ tsp **ground coriander**

¼ tsp **ground cumin**

1 tbsp **tomato paste**

FOR THE SOUP

1 medium **sweet potato**

2 cups **vegetable broth**

½ tin (200ml) **coconut milk**

100g (2 nests) **rice noodles**

½ cup (150g) **button mushrooms**, sliced

125g **Tenderstem broccoli**

1 tbsp **soy sauce** or **tamari** (adjust to taste)

½ tbsp **maple syrup** or **agave syrup**

Salt and **pepper** to taste

METHOD

FOR THE LAKSA PASTE

1. In a food processor, combine all the **laksa paste ingredients** and blend until smooth
2. To a large pot, add a little oil and the laksa paste over medium heat, and cook for about 5 minutes, stirring frequently

FOR THE SOUP

3. Peel and cube the **sweet potato** and add to the pot, sautéing for another 5 minutes
4. Pour in the **vegetable broth** and **coconut milk**, and bring the mixture to a simmer. Cook until the sweet potatoes are tender - about 15 minutes
5. Meanwhile cook the **rice noodles** to packet instructions, drain, and put to the side
6. Slice the **button mushrooms** into coins, and cut the **tenderstem broccoli** in half then add both to the pan. Let them cook until tender
7. Stir in the **soy sauce**, **maple syrup**, **salt** and **pepper** to taste
8. Divide the cooked rice noodles among serving bowls, then ladle in the laksa soup over the noodles

FINER DETAIL

To garnish, I fiercely recommend fresh coriander, spring onion, lime wedges, and sliced red chilli peppers.

For a smoother soup, feel able to use an immersion blender to reach your desired consistency.

To save time, you can also cook frozen sweet potato chunks in the oven while you make the paste and simply add them in step six with the mushrooms and broccoli.

For added protein add in crispy tofu pieces.

133

ANNA'S DUMPLING NOODLE SOUP

To my sister, and best friend, Anna. Thank you for standing alongside me with a shared commitment to people and planet - and for always making extra noodles for me.

INGREDIENTS

FOR THE DOUGH

1 cup **plain flour**

A pinch of **salt**

½ cup **warm water**

FOR THE FILLING

150g **vegan mince**

¼ **white cabbage**

2 **carrots**

2 cloves **garlic**

1 tsp ground **ginger**

1 tbsp **soy sauce**

1 tsp **sesame oil**

FOR THE SOUP

4 cups **vegetable broth**

1 tbsp **soy sauce**

1 tsp **sesame oil**

1 tsp **sriracha**

METHOD

FOR THE DOUGH

1. In a mixing bowl, combine the **flour** and **salt** and gradually add the **water**. Stir together with a fork to make the dough

2. Next, knead the dough on a floured surface for a few minutes to form a smooth ball. Cover the dough with a towel and let rest for 30 minutes

FOR THE FILLING

3. Cook the **vegan mince** in a frying pan, to packet instructions, then leave to cool

4. Finely chop the **cabbage** and **carrots**, then mince the **garlic** and grate the **ginger**, and add all these ingredients to a mixing bowl. Stir well

5. Add the vegan mince to the bowl and stir in the **soy sauce** and **sesame oil**.

BACK TO THE DOUGH

6. Roll it out on a floured surface until thin (about 3mm). Cut into half - one half will be used for the dumplings, and the other for the noodles

7. For the dumpling half, cut the dough into small squares. Fill the squares with about a tsp of the dumpling filling, then pinch the diagonal corners together and press the edges to seal

8. For the noodle half, cut the remaining dough into thin strips and dust with flour

FOR THE SOUP

9. To a large saucepan, add the **soup ingredients**, stir well and bring to a simmer. Add the noodles and dumplings for about 5 minutes, or until the dumplings float

10. Pour everything into bowls and enjoy your hearty, home-made meal!

FINER DETAIL

For some extra veggies, add some spinach or bok choy to the soup at step 9 until they wilt.

Vegan mince can be replaced by shredded tofu or vegan chick'n.

SPICY PEANUT NOODLES

Fiery and flavour-packed, these Spicy Peanut Noodles are my top choice for a speedy yet satisfying lunch.

INGREDIENTS

FOR THE SAUCE

1 tbsp **peanut butter**

1 tbsp **soy sauce**

1 tbsp **sesame oil**

1 tbsp **brown sugar**

½ tbsp **rice vinegar**

2 tsp **gochujang**

1 tsp **ground garlic**

½ tsp **ground ginger**

¼ tsp **black pepper**

FOR THE RAMEN

100g (2 nests) **ramen** or **rice noodles**

½ head **broccoli**

OPTIONAL TOPPINGS

1 **spring onion**, chopped

1 tbsp **white sesame seeds**, toasted

A handful **dry roasted peanuts**

A drizzle of **chilli oil**

METHOD

1. Mix all the **sauce ingredients** in a large bowl, and adjust the flavours to your liking

2. Cook **noodles** to packet instructions, adding the **broccoli** for the final 5 minutes

3. Drain and add immediately to the sauce bowl

4. Mix well to coat the noodles and broccoli in the spicy peanut sauce.

5. Cook on low heat for two minutes, before plating with your choice of optional toppings for extra spice and texture

FINER DETAIL

Vary the amount of gochujang (or chilli flakes) used to suit your spice tolerance.

Use a little of the noodle water to thin the sauce, if needed.

The garlic and ginger powder can be replaced by pastes or fresh grated ginger and minced garlic.

Optionally, add the dried vegetable sachet which ramen often comes with.

INDULGENT DISHES

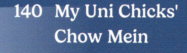

MY UNI CHICKS' CHOW MEIN

To my uni chicks, thank you for the support you gave that Chat GPT couldn't during my university experience. Soph, please don't set fire to your kitchen again when cooking this one.

INGREDIENTS

FOR THE SAUCE

2 tbsp **soy sauce**

1 tbsp **hoisin sauce**

1 tbsp **sweet chilli sauce**

2 cloves **garlic**, minced

½ tsp ground **ginger**

½ tsp **sesame oil**

FOR THE CHOW MEIN

200g **firm tofu**

3 tbsp **vegetable oil**

1 **onion**

1 red **bell pepper**

½ head **broccoli**

100g (2 nests) chow mein or ramen **noodles**

OPTIONAL TOPPINGS

1 tbsp **white sesame seeds**

2-3 **spring onions** (finely chopped)

A drizzle **sweet chilli sauce**

METHOD

1. Prepare the sauce by whisking all **sauce ingredients** together in a small bowl

2. Tear the **tofu** into small cubes and add to a large pan or wok with 2 tbsp of the **oil** over high heat.

3. Stir-fry until golden brown and crispy, then set aside

4. Prep the vegetables by dicing the **onion** and **bell pepper**, and cutting the **broccoli** into small florets

5. With the other tbsp of oil, stir-fry the vegetables until tender-crisp, for about 5 minutes

6. Cook the **noodles** according to packet instructions.

7. Drain them and add them with the tofu to the pan.

8. Pour in the sauce, coating all the ingredients and cook for a further few minutes

9. Serve the chow mein into bowls and top with the suggested **optional toppings** if desired

| Protein (g) | 19 | **25** |
| Calories (kcal) | 380 | mins |

Serves 2

FINER DETAIL

Crispy fried tofu emulates the juicy chicken you usually find in a meaty chow mein dish.

Only taking about 25 mins in total, this satisfying vegan dish will be finished faster than a takeaway.

BANANA BLOSSOM F'SH 'N CHIPS

INGREDIENTS

FOR THE BATTER

50g **plain flour**

½ cup **soy milk**

1 tbsp **white vinegar** (or pickle juice)

1 tsp **salt**

½ tsp **garlic powder**

½ tsp **onion powder**

¼ tsp **paprika**

FOR THE F'SH

1 tin (400g) **banana blossoms** in brine

50g **breadcrumbs**

¼ cup **vegetable oil** for frying

FOR THE CHIPS

2 large **russet potatoes**

Vegetable oil for frying

1 tsp **sea salt flakes**

METHOD

FOR THE BATTER

1. In a mixing bowl, whisk together all the **batter ingredients** until smooth

FOR THE F'SH

2. Lay out the **breadcrumbs** on a plate

3. Drain and rinse the **banana blossoms**, then gently pat them dry

4. Dip each piece into the batter with two forks, then press into the breadcrumbs to create the coating

5. Heat the **vegetable oil** for frying

6. Carefully place the battered f'sh into the oil and fry each side for 2-3 minutes until golden brown

7. Remove the f'sh with a slotted spoon and place them on a paper towel-lined plate to drain the excess oil. Set aside while you prepare the chips

| Protein (g) | 5 | **30** |
| Calories (kcal) | 450 | mins |

Serves 2

FOR THE CHIPS

8. Slice the **potatoes** into chips, add to the **oil** and fry for about 5-10 minutes until golden and crispy

9. Place on new paper towels and sprinkle with **salt** while they're hot

10. Plate the f'sh and chips while hot, and enjoy!

FINER DETAIL

Serve with pickles, vegan mayo, mushy peas and salt and vinegar for the ultimate experience.

Use chickpea flour for a gluten free option.

Fry both the f'sh and chips in small batches if needed, depending on pan size.

Use an air-fryer to reduce the calories.

CAULIFLOWER BUFFALO WINGS

INGREDIENTS

½ head **cauliflower**

150g **breadcrumbs**

FOR THE BATTER

2 cups (240g) **plain flour**

1 tsp **paprika**

2 tsp **garlic salt**

½ tsp **pepper**

2 tbsp **nutritional yeast**

600ml **unsweetened plant milk**

FOR THE DRIZZLE

½ cup (110g) of **vegan butter**

1 tbsp **sriracha**

½ tsp **garlic salt**

FOR THE CRUDITÉS

2 **carrots**

½ **cucumber**

4 **celery** sticks

METHOD

FOR THE WINGS & DRIZZLE

1. Preheat the oven to 180°C. Line a large oven tray with baking paper

2. In a large bowl, combine the **flour**, **paprika**, **garlic salt**, **pepper**, and **nutritional yeast** and whisk

3. Then gradually whisk in the **plant milk** to create the batter

4. Cut the **cauliflower** into small florets

5. Pour the **breadcrumbs** into a separate bowl

6. Using two forks, coat the cauliflower pieces in the batter then the breadcrumbs and place on the baking tray. Cook for 20 minutes

7. In a small microwavable bowl melt the **butter** on a low heat setting in the microwave

8. Mix in the **sriracha** and **garlic salt** and drizzle the mixture over the cauliflower before cooking for a futher 20 minutes

FOR THE CRUDITÉS

9. Peel the **carrots** and slice them, along with the **cucumber** and **celery,** into batons

10. Serve with the cauliflower buffalo wings along with sauces of your choice

| Protein (g) | 18 | **15** |
| Calories (kcal) | 280 | mins |

+40 minutes baking time
Serves 2

FINER DETAIL

You can either buy
premade breadcrumbs
or tear about 3 to 4
slices of bread into a
food processor and make
them yourself.

I enjoy sriracha
mayo or
more of
the
drizzle.

145

KOREAN FRIED CHICK'N AND CHIPS

INGREDIENTS

FOR THE CHICK'N AND COATING

¼ cup **vegetable oil**, for frying

½ cup **plain flour**

½ cup **cornflour**

1 tsp **garlic salt**

1 tsp **onion powder**

1 tsp **paprika**

160g **vegan chick'n pieces**

FOR THE CHIPS

2 **large potatoes**

1 tsp **salt**

FOR THE SAUCE

½ cup **soy sauce**

1 tbsp **agave syrup**

1 tbsp **rice vinegar**

1 tsp **sesame oil**

2 cloves **garlic**

½ tsp **ground ginger**

1 tbsp **gochujang**

1 tsp **cornflour**

METHOD

FOR THE CHICK'N AND COATING

1. Heat the **oil** in a deep frying pan or a deep fryer to 175-190°C

2. In a shallow bowl, mix together the **flour**, **cornflour**, **garlic salt**, **onion powder** and **paprika**

3. Coat the **chick'n pieces** in the flour mixture then add to the hot oil and fry until golden brown (about 5 minutes). Remove and drain on paper towels to catch the excess oil

FOR THE CHIPS

4. Slice the **potatoes** into chips, then add to the oil and fry for about 5-10 minutes until golden and crispy. Place on new paper towels and sprinkle with the **salt** while hot

FOR THE SAUCE

5. In a separate bowl, whisk together the **sauce ingredients**, leaving the **cornflour** until last

6. Toss the chick'n in the sauce until each piece is coated, and cook until hot in a separate frying pan

TO SERVE

7. Serve the Korean Fried Chick'n alongside the chips. Garnish with spring onions, sesame seeds, and sauces of your choosing

| Protein (g) | 48 | **40** |
| Calories (kcal) | 615 | mins |

Serves 2

FINER DETAIL

As seen in the photo, I sometimes use dehydrated 'meats' as you can buy them in bulk so they're often cheaper.

To avoid deep-frying, air fry the chick'n and chips separately or bake the chips in the oven at 190°C for 30 minutes or so and pan fry the chick'n.

DESSERTS

BEN'S BANOFFEE PIE

BenJAMIN, your love for hearty cakes, pies and all things sweet surpasses all else. I look forward to many more baking sessions with you and our tunes.

INGREDIENTS

Makes 12 pieces

FOR THE BUTTERY BISCUIT BASE

250g pack **lotus biscuits**

80g **vegan butter**

FOR THE CARAMEL

50g **vegan butter**

50g **light brown sugar**

370g tin **vegan condensed milk**

25g **cornflour**

50ml **sweetened soy milk**

TO TOP

1 sliced **banana**

1 tin **vegan whipped cream**

60g **dark chocolate**

METHOD

FOR THE BUTTERY BISCUIT BASE

1. Crush the **biscuits** using a zip-lock bag and a rolling pin (it's quite therapeutic). Pour into a bowl.

2. Melt the **butter** in a small saucepan then pour into the bowl and stir with a wooden spoon to combine

3. Transfer the mixture into a cupcake tray and leave in the fridge to chill while you make the caramel

FOR THE CARAMEL

4. Melt the **butter** in a saucepan, then stir in the **sugar** and **condensed milk** and increase to medium heat. Cook, stirring constantly, until the mixture bubbles

5. Turn the heat to high, gradually whisk in the **cornflour**, then the **soy milk.** Boil for 5-10 minutes, or until the caramel is deep brown

6. Remove the base from the fridge and pour in the caramel. Chill the pies for an hour

TO SERVE

7. Cover the pies with the sliced **banana**, then **whipped cream**

8. Grate on the **dark chocolate** and serve immediately

FINER DETAIL

You can also follow this method using a cake tin, and make one large pie.

The cream topping means the recipe needs to be served quite quickly. You could even place the whipped cream can on the side and allow guests to serve themselves.

Without the toppings the pie will last 3-5 days refrigerated.

ANUM'S CHOCOLATE CHUNK COOKIES

BEWARE: these are incredibly moreish. This recipe has been tried and tested many, many times by my friend Anum and I, so this one's for you Noom :))

INGREDIENTS

110g **vegan butter**

150g **light brown sugar**

50g caster **sugar**

3 tbsp **aquafaba**

2 tsp **vanilla essence**

310g plain **flour**

1 tsp **baking powder**

1 tsp **salt**

1 tsp **bicarbonate of soda**

150g **vegan chocolate**

FINER DETAIL

Aquafaba is the water that chickpeas come in and is a great egg replacer. You can get it from brands like Oggs™ or from the tin (chickpeas can be saved for my Red Thai or Creamy Hummus and Crispy Chickpea recipes).

For thick cookies, I recommend 60g per ball, otherwise aim for 50g.

METHOD

To make a batch of roughly 10 cookies

1. Preheat your oven to 180°C and line two large baking trays

2. Whisk together the **butter** (at room temperature) and **sugars** to get a fluffy mixture

3. Add in the **aquafaba** and **vanilla essence** and whisk until combined

4. Next, whisk in the **flour**, **baking powder**, **salt**, and **bicarbonate of soda**

5. Chop the **vegan chocolate** into small chunks and fold these into the mixture

6. Roll the mixture into balls, then place them onto the baking trays leaving enough space between the cookies. I place 5 on each tray and lightly press the balls down

7. Bake for 12 minutes and leave to cool for at least 10 minutes, before scoffing the lot!

152

CHOCOLATE PEANUT CUPS

INGREDIENTS

Makes 10 pieces

1 cup **oat bran** (or blended oats)

2 tbsp **peanut butter**

1 tsp **Biscoff spread**

½ cup **maple syrup**

A pinch of **salt**

1 tbsp **chocolate spread**

10g **peanuts**

50g **vegan chocolate**

2 tbsp **coconut oil**

a pinch of **salt flakes**

FINER DETAIL

Use agave syrup instead of maple syrup for a cheaper option.

You can also melt the chocolate in a water bath (in a heatproof bowl on top of boiling water.)

METHOD

1. In a bowl, combine the **oat bran**, **peanut butter**, **Biscoff spread**, **maple syrup** and **salt**

2. Spoon the mixture into a greased cupcake tray, then make a small hole in each and fill with half a tsp of **chocolate spread** and a few **peanuts**

3. Next break up the **vegan chocolate** into chunks and place in a microwaveable bowl with the **coconut oil**

4. Microwave for 30 seconds on medium heat. Stir well and continue to microwave in 30-second intervals until chocolate is melted

5. Pour the melted chocolate into the cupcake trays until each cup is covered, and gently add the peanuts to the top

6. Place in the fridge for at least an hour before adding **salt flakes**

BANANA BREAD

INGREDIENTS

Makes 8-10 slices

3 ripe **bananas**

½ cup **coconut oil**, melted

3 tbsp of **aquafaba**

¼ cup **maple syrup**

1 tsp **vanilla extract**

1½ cups **plain flour**

1 tsp **baking powder**

½ tsp **bicarbonate of soda**

½ tsp **salt**

1 tsp **cinnamon**

½ tsp **nutmeg**

FINER DETAIL

Fold in any additional mix-ins like nuts, vegan chocolate or dried fruit at step 5.

If adding vegan chocolate chips to the batter, I recommend setting some aside to add to the top after step 6, just before baking.

METHOD

1. Preheat the oven to 180°C and line or grease a 9-inch loaf tin

2. In a large mixing bowl, mash the **bananas** with a fork until smooth

3. Whisk in the melted **coconut oil**, **aquafaba**, **maple syrup**, and **vanilla extract** until well combined

4. In a separate bowl, whisk together the **flour**, **baking powder**, **bicarbonate of soda**, **salt**, **cinnamon** and **nutmeg**

5. Add the **dry ingredients** to the **wet ingredients** and stir to create a batter, but avoid overmixing

6. Pour the batter into the loaf tin and smooth out the top with a spoon or spatula

7. Bake the banana bread for about 45 minutes, or until a toothpick inserted into the center comes out clean

8. Let it cool for 10 minutes in the tin and then 10 further minutes on a wire rack before slicing and serving

Per slice (for 8)

Protein (g)	2.6
Calories (kcal)	263

30 mins

+ 45 minutes baking

157

CHOCOLATE CARAMEL BARS

INGREDIENTS

Makes 20 pieces

FOR THE BASE

1 cup **almond flour**

½ cup **oat flour**

¼ cup **coconut oil**, melted

2 tbsp **maple syrup**

¼ tsp **salt**

FOR THE CARAMEL

½ cup **Biscoff spread** (or any vegan cookie spread)

2 tbsp **coconut oil**

1 tsp **vanilla extract**

FOR THE CHOCOLATE TOPPING

120g **vegan chocolate** (chips or chopped)

2 tbsp **coconut oil**

1 tsp **sea salt flakes**

FINER DETAIL

If you are (like me) impatient when it comes to chocolate, freeze where it says refrigerate, for half the time.

This recipe is not only vegan, but also gluten free!

158

Per Bar

Protein (g)	2	**15** mins
Calories (kcal)	167	

+ an hour refrigeration
makes 20 pieces

METHOD

FOR THE BASE

1. In a bowl, mix together the **almond flour**, **oat flour**, melted **coconut oil**, **maple syrup**, and **salt** until well combined
2. Press the mixture firmly into the base of a lined pan or dish (about 8x8 inches or similar)

FOR THE CARAMEL

3. In a microwave-safe bowl, or in a saucepan on the stovetop, melt the **Biscoff spread** and **coconut oil** together until smooth
4. Stir in the **vanilla extract**, then poor the mixture over the base
5. Place the pan in the refrigerator to set the caramel layer for about a half hour

FOR THE CHOCOLATE TOPPING

6. Then, melt the **vegan chocolate** with the **coconut oil** in a microwave-safe bowl or in a saucepan on the stovetop, stirring often, until smooth
7. Pour the melted chocolate over the caramel layer, spreading it evenly
8. Lastly, refrigerate for about half an hour, or until the chocolate is firm. Sprinkle with the **sea salt flakes**, cut into bars and enjoy!

CHOCOLATE PRETZEL BARK

INGREDIENTS

75g **pretzels**

210g **vegan chocolate chips/chunks**

20g **rice crispies**

½ tsp **sea salt flakes**

FINER DETAIL

The bark should be about 2 cm thick, so choose your tray size accordingly.

Other toppings could include sprinkles, crushed biscuits, nuts or a caramel sauce.

For a festive twist use mint chocolate and add candy canes. The chocolate bark can then be packaged and gifted too!

If you'd like the pretzels to be more visible, gently press them in at step 3.

METHOD

1. Line a baking tray with baking paper, and place the **pretzels** in an even layer - you can choose to crush the pretzels if you want smaller pieces at this step

2. Melt the **vegan chocolate** in the microwave or in a double boiler and pour it over the pretzels. The chocolate should fill the pretzel holes and create a smooth layer.

3. While the chocolate is still melted, sprinkle over the **rice crispies** and **sea salt flakes**

4. Refrigerate for about an hour or in the freezer for 20-30 minutes.

5. Remove from the fridge, break off pieces from the tray and serve

NATHAN'S MICROWAVE CHOCOLATE CAKE

To my broski, this one - unsurprisingly - is for you. Unlike the first attempt you suffered through, this cake is light, rich and fluffy, and packed with enough sugar to get you through your last minute assignments or even a daring D&D game.

INGREDIENTS

For one large mug cake

4 tbsp **cocoa powder**

7 tbsp **plain flour**

½ tsp **baking powder**

50g **vegan chocolate chips/ chunks**

a pinch of **salt**

6 tbsp **soy milk**

4 tbsp **maple syrup**

2 tbsp **vegetable oil**

1 tsp **vanilla extract**

FINER DETAIL

You can eat the cake directly from the mug or transfer it to a bowl. Optionally serve with a scoop of vegan ice cream or custard and a dusting of icing sugar.

Experiment with different mix-ins like chopped nuts, dried fruits, nut butters, or even vegan marshmallows.

Protein (g)	8	**10**
Calories (kcal)	350	mins

Serves 1

METHOD

1. First, combine the dry ingredients in a mug: the **cocoa powder**, **flour**, **baking powder**, **chocolate chips** and **salt**

2. Next gradually pour in the wet ingredients: the **soy milk**, **maple syrup**, **oil**, and **vanilla extract**

3. Stir well to combine

4. Microwave for 1-2 minutes on 900W. The cake should have risen and look set but still be slightly moist on top when done

5. Allow to cool for a few minutes before serving

DOUBLE CHOCOLATE PROTEIN BALLS

INGREDIENTS

2 cups **oat flour**

1 scoop (30g) chocolate **protein powder**

A pinch of **salt**

½ cup **vegan chocolate chunks** or chips

½ cup **coconut oil**

1/3 cup **maple syrup**

FINER DETAIL

You can make your own oat flour by blending oats in a food processor for under a minute or so.

I enjoy these on their own pre or post-workout, or as a dessert with a vegan chocolate pot or custard.

Optionally dust with extra cocoa powder.

METHOD

1. To a large mixing bowl, add the dry ingredients: the **oat flour, protein powder, salt** and **chocolate chunks**. Stir well with a wooden spoon

2. Melt the **coconut oil** in the microwave on low heat for 30 seconds or in a saucepan

3. Gradually pour the melted coconut oil and **maple syrup** into the bowl. Mix to combine until it has a slightly crumbly texture, but still clumps together in places

4. Roll the mixture into small balls. They are ready to eat, and can be stored in the refrigerator

Per Protein Ball

Protein (g)	5.3	**15** mins
Calories (kcal)	350	

Makes 30 Protein balls

Date Night Delights

DATE NIGHT DELIGHTS

INGREDIENTS

12 **Medjool dates**

6 tbsp **peanut butter**

75g vegan **chocolate chips** or chopped vegan chocolate

1 tsp **coconut oil**

½ tsp **sea salt flakes** (optional)

OPTIONAL FILLINGS

Peanuts, **pistachios**, **almonds** or **cashews**

Shredded **coconut**

FINER DETAIL

I sometimes make these without the chocolate to eat before a run for a light energy boost.

These last in the fridge for 1-2 weeks, and can last for up to 2-3 months frozen.

Optionally drizzle on some peanut butter before sprinkling on the salt flakes, as seen in the picture.

METHOD

1. Preheat your oven to 175°C

2. Make a small lengthwise slit in each **Medjool date** to remove the pit without splitting the date open completely

3. Stuff each date with about half a tsp of **peanut butter** and any other of the **optional fillings**

4. Place the stuffed dates on a lined baking tray and roast for 5 minutes to slightly caramelize them

5. Remove from the oven and leave to cool

6. Meanwhile, melt the **vegan chocolate** with the **coconut oil** in a microwave-safe bowl or in a saucepan on the stovetop, stirring often, until smooth

7. Using two forks, carefully coat each stuffed date in the melted chocolate

8. Place the chocolate-covered dates back on the lined baking tray, sprinkle on the **salt flakes**, and set in the fridge for about 15 minutes before serving

Per Date

		20 mins
Protein (g)	3.5	
Calories (kcal)	249	

+ 15 minutes refrigeration
Serves 6

AMY'S SPICED MAPLE AND PECAN MONKEY BREAD

To my dear friend Amy, who has shared in the story of my life, with parts that drift and return, growing alongside me. To baking sessions and a continued friendship.

INGREDIENTS

FOR THE DOUGH

½ cup luke warm **soy milk**

¼ cup luke warm **water**

7g **active dry yeast**

¼ cup melted **vegan butter**

¼ cup **maple syrup**

1 tsp **vanilla extract**

½ tsp **cinnamon**

¼ tsp **nutmeg**

¼ tsp **allspice**

3 cups **plain flour**

½ tsp **salt**

FOR THE COATING

1 cup **light brown sugar**

1 tsp **cinnamon**

FOR THE ASSEMBLY

1/3 cup melted **vegan butter**

1 cup **chopped pecans**

FOR THE MAPLE GLAZE

½ cup **icing sugar**

½ tsp **water**

2 tbsp **maple syrup**

FINER DETAIL

Thoroughly grease your pan!

During assembly, don't worry about any gaps between the dough balls - these are filled during rising.

This is best eaten on the day it's made, but can be wrapped and stored for 24 hours. Reheat the next day, in the oven, on a low heat.

Per Serving

Protein (g)	3.9
Calories (kcal)	350

Preparation **20** mins

Cooking **30** mins

+ 90 minutes rising

Serves 12

METHOD

FOR THE DOUGH

1. In a bowl, combine the warm **soy milk** and warm **water**. Sprinkle the **yeast** over the liquid and let it sit for about 5 minutes until frothy

2. Add melted **vegan butter**, **maple syrup**, **vanilla extract**, and **all the spices** to the yeast mixture

3. Mix well, then gradually mix in the **flour** and **salt** until a sticky dough forms

4. Turn the dough onto a floured surface and knead for about 5 minutes until smooth and elastic

5. Place the dough in a greased bowl, cover with a damp cloth, and let it rise for about 1 hour

Please Turn Over

AMY'S SPICED MAPLE AND PECAN MONKEY BREAD

FOR THE COATING AND ASSEMBLY

6. Meanwhile, in a separate bowl, mix together the **sugar** and **cinnamon**

7. Punch down the dough and divide it into roughly golf-ball-sized pieces

8. Dip each piece into the melted **vegan butter**, then roll it in the cinnamon-sugar until coated

9. Place a layer of coated dough balls in a greased Bundt pan or round cake pan. Flatten each piece slightly to provide a base for a layer of chopped **pecans**. Repeat with another layer of dough and pecans until all the dough is used

FINAL RISE AND BAKING

10. Cover the pan with a damp cloth and let the dough balls rise for another 30 minutes, Towards the end of this time, preheat the oven to 175°C

11. Bake the monkey bread for 25-30 minutes, or until the top is golden brown and the bread is cooked through (check with a toothpick)

MAPLE GLAZE

12. Prepare the maple glaze by mixing the **glaze ingredients** together

13. Once baked, let the monkey bread cool for at least 10 minutes before carefully turning the pan upside-down and removing the contents

14. Lastly, drizzle over the maple glaze and serve. The bread can be sliced and served, or for more fun you can tear it apart piece by piece

ABOUT THE BOOK

The concept, text and the majority of the photos[†] of *The Plantary Cookbook* were created by Ellen Barrett.

It is set in Gelica, a typeface designed by Dave Rowland (of the foundry Eclectotype) to be friendly and approachable.

This book was designed by Simon Barrett of *Quirky Ink*, a new publishing house, focusing on works which have scope for a little pizzazz in their design.

The Plantary Cookbook is the first book published by Quirky Ink.

It was printed in A5, on 130 gsm paper by PixartPrinting, Venice, Italy.

ABOUT THE AUTHOR

The Plantary Cookbook is written by up-and-coming environmental entrepreneur, Ellen Barrett:
- vegan recipe creator
- post-grad in Climate Change Studies
- garlic salt enthusiast

Her passion for accesible vegan cooking is clear in every recipe, making it easy for everyone to 'plant' their forks into something scrumptious.

Follow her on Instagam to keep up to date...

#the.plantary_

INDEX